NEGOTIATING FOR LIFE

Wit, Wisdom & Strategies

for Your Success

JB Shelton-Spurr

Dedicated to

Harvey Spurr, my husband

John Baker, The Negotiator Magazine,
negotiatormagazine.com, my editor

Professional Negotiating Skills,
Transforming Life's Challenges
into Win-Win Results,
Osher Lifelong Learning Institute
Duke University,
my students

Introduction

JB Shelton-Spurr shares advice from Shakespeare, Winston Churchill, Alice in Wonderland, Abraham Lincoln and Scarlett O'Hara.

JB touches upon her careers as a journalist, artist's agent and cattle rancher.

She teaches *Professional Negotiating Skills: Transforming Life's Challenges into Win-Win Results* at Osher Lifelong Learning Institute at Duke University. JB is contributing editor of *The Negotiator Magazine,* negotiatormagazine.com

Publishing History

Articles (c) 2011-2014
JB Shelton-Spurr
and
The Negotiator Magazine

Table of Contents

1 Learning to Love to Negotiate

The title *Learning to Love to Negotiate* may strike you as intriguing and ridiculous. Negotiating is complex and challenging. It requires hours, days, weeks of research, preparation and organization before the negotiation even begins.

Every negotiation is different. Although we learn from experience, we can never be absolutely certain about the next outcome. If we dislike hard work and surprise endings, hating to negotiate is more likely than loving it.

What is there, you may rightly inquire, to love about negotiating? Oh, let me count my personal ways of thinking and doing that lead me to love being a professional negotiator.

Everything is Under Control

When I think about loving to negotiate, my mentor's mantra comes to mind: "Everything is under control." I understand the phrase as a mindset, not a literal interpretation.

Every negotiation inspires me to assess my natural abilities, skills and talents. I contemplate, then plan, how to maximize control over the various aspects of my next negotiation. I consider how to effectively apply my experiences in previously successful negotiations to my new challenges.

My purpose is to renew self-confidence, synergize competencies, and turn attributes into creative, logical, powerful actions. Such actions inevitably dissipate my fears, anger and hesitancy.

Motivating Factor

Every essential negotiation has a primary motivating factor that inspires. In a blaze of stream-of-consciousness, describe that factor in a clarifying, summarizing sentence. Determine why you are passionate about winning. Focus on how your career, prosperity, personal life, community involvement or other areas will benefit you, your family, friends, neighbors, business colleagues.

If you cannot state why it's essential, declare the negotiation non-essential. You cannot love wasting time and energy on something that needn't be done: Don't do it.

It's Not Personal

I've discovered that being objective about myself is an excellent way to decrease stress and increase my enjoyment of negotiating. I admire, apply and therefore share these recommendations to lighten up about emotional responses. Treat the business of negotiating as a business matter. Remember not to take interactions personally.

Executive coach Brian Koslow advised, "During a negotiation, it would be wise not to take anything personally. If you leave personalities out of it, you will be able to see opportunities more objectively."

Watergate-era politician Howard Baker, declared, "The most difficult thing in any negotiation is making sure that you strip it of the emotion and deal with the facts."

Felix Dennis, British publisher, poet, philanthropist, stated, "You have to persuade yourself that you absolutely don't care what happens. I promise you, in every serious negotiation, the man or woman who doesn't care is going to win."

Approach-Avoidance Conflicts

Stress is inherent in negotiating interactions. Kurt Lewin, a founder of modern social psychology, defined approach-avoidance conflicts as stressful. When we take the approach that a negotiation holds a true and valued purpose, loving to negotiate comes to fruition.

Lewin defined avoidance as being fearful, suspicious, anticipating negatively, misdirecting mental and emotional energy. The brave soul looks inward to examine the negative (avoidance) aspects. She seeks to understand why certain thoughts are illogical and worth discarding.

Incentives and Research

You don't need extrasensory perception to follow Americanentrepreneur Eli Broad's advice: "The best move you can make in negotiation is to think of an incentive the other person hasn't even thought of and then meet it." I love the detective work, the creative thinking, the aha! moments on the path to discovering my opponent's incentive.

How, indeed, do you conjure up that vital incentive? It's a matter of knowing your opponent's history, strengths and goals almost as well as you know your own. You will be able to feel a pleasurable, ego-satisfying measure of control when you invest creativity, time and talent in researching beyond corporate annual reports, *Wall Street Journal* articles, and PBS *Nightly Business Report* features.

I take advantage of the professional and personal revelations available on LinkedIn, the world's largest professional network, boasting 250 million members. The profiles are compendia of careers, skills, advocations, publications, memberships and awards, all well worth researching and following up with our mutual contacts for more information.

Natural Negotiators

Some folks just come naturally to getting their way. Adorable toddlers. Corporate bigwigs awarded golden parachutes. Charismatic televangelists. Three a.m. tv infomercial hosts.

Visualize yourself as achieving your negotiating goals with professionalism. Your demeanor, image and attitude are secure. You take pleasure, not in destroying your opponent, but in holding a negotiation that achieves your goal and provides a measure of success for him.

The more you negotiate successfully, the more you will think of yourself as blessed with the powers of being a natural negotiator. Realizing you love to negotiate is worthy of celebrating youself.

2 *Negotiating with Yourself*

Pillow Talk

You begin every day negotiating with yourself.

From the first mellifluous tones of your classical music station, or that strange alarm designed to fall off your bedside table and bounce about the room as it gets louder and louder.

You begin every day negotiating with yourself. Applying the 'Do I really?' test gets those early morning mental and physical kinks out of the way, although adding a hot shower and aromatic cup of deep roast coffee do their part.

Self Reflections

Negotiating with (not for or by or in spite of) yourself is as complicated as negotiating with someone else. Perhaps, moreso. Our most challenging negotiations are all too often with ourselves.

The wisdom of 'know thyself' is transformed into the reality of 'no, myself.' That face in the mirror stubbornly refuses to smile back. We take every part of life seriously, whether or not the occasion is deserving.

We all-or-nothing, think black-or-white, demand always-or-never, as if our lives were destined to fit into a perfect world and anything less won't suffice.

Do I Really...?

Many decisions take micro-milliseconds. Others are lifelong battles. Most fit neatly in the middle of controllable actions. Asking ourselves, 'Do I really...?,' is a key to making wise decisions. It self-enlightens to differentiate between our perpetual angel-on-one-shoulder, devil-on-the-other, wants versus needs.

The BBC Reporter

On a National Public Radio broadcast, a BBC reporter talked calmly about his assignments in the Middle East. He detailed the professional thrill of researching and investigating major stories, interacting with folks he'd remember for the rest of his life, broadcasting the results to enlighten BBC listeners worldwide.

Meeting confidential sources in back alleys in the black of night became second nature. He had (I imagine), asked himself, 'Do I really want to put my life at risk for my career?' and responded with a resounding 'Yes!' In his words, 'Sometimes getting shot at is a bit of a bother.' A sense of humor will get you far.

HALTS

Here's a simple lifesaver, especially helpful when you can't figure out why you can't decide. Are you hungry, angry, lonely, tired, scared or a combination within the quintet? The five cover a multitude of self-destructive sins.

Release yourself from the anxieties of the decision-making mode. Think about what you're suffering from and simply do something positive about each. You're negotiating with yourself for good mental, emotional and physical health.

Be Your Own Hero

You've met him: That tough negotiator who has only his own interests at heart. He asks for what he wants and wants what he asks for. His patience level is so low that requiring him to wait a minute causes a glaring stare.

He has a history of negotiating success and no qualms about revealing his triumphs. He is intimidating, never having to yield for permission from a higher authority. He makes up his mind and never budges. He isn't looking for a friend, making small talk or concerned about what you think about him.

Don't you wish you could be just like him? Or, perhaps, a kinder, gentler, but still as effective version of him? Do some of his 'attributes' repulse you, while others evoke your envy?

Your Negotiating with Yourself Assignment

Treat yourself as if your very life depended on your abilities to negotiate with yourself -- to know and keep your own best interests in heart and mind. Don't jump: Glide.

Honor the praise FOCI, FLOW, FRUITION. What are you determined to accomplish?

How are you setting up your life to prioritize and take actions that will make the day disappear with resultant proof of productivity and feelings of accomplishment?

Be determined to celebrate yourself when you've reached fruition and are ready to start the cycle over and over again?

3 Intuitive Negotiating

Who do your trust? If your immediate reaction was *myself*, you're blessed. You have a natural proclivity toward intuitive negotiating.

Do you consider your decisive actions based on intuition to be courageous moves? Congratulations: They are, indeed.

Courage of Your Contradictions

Negotiation gurus expound upon the need for copious research and planning as pre-determiners of how you'll succeed in a negotiation.. They do not often give credit or credence to that little voice in the back of your head that, curiously enough, can serve as the logical and final influence on your decisions.

Examine your positive experiences in negotiations where your intuition may have overridden your logic and research, and nonetheless brought about your success. Consider whether you were fortunate in a rare instance or can proudly point out noteworthy experiences.

Sharing your negotiating successes, where intuition brought about good results, is an excellent technique for transforming those questioning stares into agreeable team spirit.

"Trust me, I just know," will not automatically inspire your colleagues' confidence. Intuition can elucidate the crowning moments of individual stages of a negotiaton. Your intuition is, of course, intertwined with facts you've absorbed and decisions you're made. It is one vital part of a multi-faceted decision-making process.

Meeting of the Minds

As an interim step, ask your colleagues to tap into their own intuitions about the current negotiation. If there's a meeting of the minds/guts, go with it. Let them share professional examples of their intuitive successes as well.

Chances are, members of your negotiating team have used intuition successfully to solve problems and move issues along when they were not in a formal negotiating situation. Those instances, too, will provide more comfortable and enthusiastic reactions to using intuition in the meeting room.

Art and Science

Negotiating is both an art and a science. Intuition logically belongs in the art category, being more creative, imaginative and feeling-based than the science of fact gathering, analyzing and organizing.

Fixation on the facts can distract from attempts to negotiate intuitively. Playing the objective observer will enhance your ability to get in touch with your intuitive side.

Getting in touch with your intuition is mental, emotional and physical. Your mental mindset needs to be relaxed, receptive and inventive. Your emotional baggage must be unpacked.

Your physical tightness and tension require taking time to exercise your body, calm down, breathe deeply and meditate to feel peacefully focused.

 If you are in the daily habit of walking or running, you may experience an intuitive aha! moment of clarity at the end of your workout.

Suspecting Your Intuition is Incorrect

When is it wise not to rely on your intuition?:

When you have not fully explored all the facts
When you are emotionally involved, not thinking clearly
When you feel afraid or unsure about making a decision
When you're involved in a deadlocked situation and just
  want a conclusion

Body Language and Mindreading

Knowing how to read your opponents' body language can
provide a wealth of information for your intuition. Explore
beyond his words to the confidence he shows or doesn't
show – poor posture, lack of eye contact, fidgety body parts
Let your intuition tell you whether you are in a stronger
position than you thought you were; do not hesitate to
increase your demands.

Women's Intuition

An insightful description of intuition comes from
commentator Abella Arthur. "Intuition is a combination of
historical (empirical) data, deep and heightened observation,
and an ability to cut through the thickness of surface reality.

Intuition is like a slow motion machine that captures data
instantaneously and hits you like a ton of bricks. Intuition is a
knowing, a sensing that is beyond the conscious
understanding: a gut feeling. Intuition is not pseudo-science."

Ms. Arthur and I make no claims that as women our intuitive powers outshine those of the male gender. I firmly believe, however, that females are more in touch with the emotional aspects of life, particularly in communicating with other people. Valuable to intuitive abilities is the ability to listen, to care enough to consider what someone is talking about, and to listen to head and heart in responding.

4 Virtues of Integrity

Plato

"There is nothing so delightful as the hearing or the speaking of truth. For this reason, there is no conversation so agreeable as that of a man of integrity, who hears without any intention to betray, and speaks without any intention to deceive," wrote Plato.

The Greek philosopher, who lived from 427 to 347 BC, provides a perfect description of the modern negotiator with an innate dedication to a personal moral imperative.

Pursue and Persevere

Integrity is a strict adherence to a moral code of honesty and harmony in thoughts, words and actions. It means possessing firm principles and professional standards. The word's Latin derivation refers to being sound and whole.

It is essential to face the reality that negotiating with integrity is a challenge worth pursuit and perseverance. Determine your foci and work diligently as the flow of your efforts reach fruition.

It is who you are, as your consistent better self goes beyond negotiations into all your life's priorities.

The Principled Negotiator

The principled negotiator strives for success by self-examination. She proves to herself and to others that having a conscience is not an endangered position. Answering these questions will provide insights, from logical and comforting to revealing and surprising:

What does having integrity mean to you as a negotiator?
How strongly do you value communications and
interactions based on honesty?
Is your behavior consistent toward your opponents?

Dangerous and Dreadful

"Integrity without knowledge is weak and useless, and knowledge without integrity is dangerous and dreadful," wrote 18th century English author Samuel Johnson.

As you prepare for your next negotiation, keep your answers to the self-examination questions in mind and heart. Mentally review a recent, successful negotiation and admit to yourself where your integrity was lacking, how you over-reacted in responding to your opponent, and when you broke the bond of your own principles.

Follow through on your commitment. Re-examine yourself for the next negotiation and those to follow. Mentally commit to changes that will enhance your integrity.

Skeptical, not Cynical

"Confidence in others' honesty is no light testimony of one's own integrity," wrote 16th century French philosopher Michel de Montaigne. Journalism school students are taught to be skeptical, not cynical. The classic example is, "If your mother says she loves you, check out two other sources."

Researching your opponent will reveal basic facts and fictions, give an historical perspective about his previous negotiations, and provide insights into his negotiating style.

Enter a negotiation fully prepared to believe your opponent, but allow your suspicions to linger when his statements, written materials and body language strike you as less than the epitome of honesty.

Be thoughtful, patient and judicious before bringing up your doubts about his veracity. If you decide his honesty is an issue, communicate directly and specifically, without accusation and anger.

Integrity Without Game Playing

"Nothing more completely baffles one who is full of tricks and duplicity than straightforward and simple integrity," wrote 18th century English cleric Charles Caleb Colton.

Oh, the games we professional negotiators play. Pretending to appeal to a higher authority when we have final say.

Communicating to confuse rather than clarify. Arranging a phone call to interrupt a meeting and apologetically fleeing the scene to garner more time.

Carefully consider the games you often play because you've found them successful. They may appear to be essential components of your performance as a successful negotiator. Think creatively about ways to replace the games with equally effective negotiating techniques. If you make a conscious decision to keep the games in your repertoire, realize you are being honest -- but only with yourself.

Visionaries

Two 20th century visionaries provide further inspiration for you to negotiate with integrity and live with a joyful awareness of your self worth.

Buddhist leader Daisaku Ikeda said, "When you live with integrity, your hearts begin to fill with a happiness as vast as the universe. It's about being true to yourself and starting from where you are."

English photographer Sir Cecil Beaton wrote, "Be daring, be different, be impractical, be anything that will assert integrity of purpose and imaginative vision against the play-it-safers, the creatures of commonplace, the victims of ordinary."

Become your own visionary. Envision your reputation as a negotiator who is respected and admired for his integrity.

5 Inner Peaceful Negotiating

Your ego, career, finances and health are excellent reasons to seek inner peace when negotiating. Imagine creating a mind and body with mental, emotional and physical resilience.

Heart pounding, inability to concentrate and sleepless nights are associated with stress, anxiety and panic. Peace of mind is associated with bliss, happiness and contentment. You have a choice about how you act and react.

By lessening your stress level, you will be mentally and physically able to focus on preparing for and conducting negotiations. And you will have the concentration and energy to increase successful outcomes.

Mind Your Business: Business Your Mind

Your next highly anticipated negotiation may not affect world peace, childhood hunger or economic stability. However, it is vital to remember how important that negotiation is to you:

Will the results dramatically change your life?
Will a win-win conclusion be sufficient to satisfy you?
Will you give more time and energy than necessary to negotiate successfully?

Self-preservation necessitates being positively self-centered, not in an egotistical manner, but by thinking through what you want and don't want from a negotiation.

Zen and Relaxation Response

In the sixth century BC, Zen Buddhists in China practiced meditation to study their own minds and understand the nature of their thought processes. Their purpose was to lessen stress by coming face-to-face with themselves as individuals in an intimate and direct way.

The *don't know mind* is a Zen principle designed to let the practitioner maintain ideas while letting go of personal attachment to them.

In 1976, a book titled *The Relaxation Response* by Herbert Benson, M.D., was destined to translate the Zen practices into 20th century practices and become an international bestseller for decades. Dr. Benson, associate professor of medicine at Harvard Medical School and founder of the Mind Body Medical Institute, describes the relaxation response as "a physical state of deep rest that changes the physical and emotional resonses to stress. It is the opposite of our fight or flight response."

Meditation -- ancient Zen Buddhism and modern Relaxation Response – share a focus on taking a comfortable position, breathing deeply, and repeating a single word or simple phrase, beginning with a ten-minute sesion, to evoke a relaxed mental and physical consciousness of the present. Both create a fresh start, a clear and calm attitude, a relaxed body, an ability to prioritize and plan, and a sense of having life under control.

Fear of Fearing

It is only by taking actions that expand and clarify our thoughts and motivate us to take care of ourselves that we can conquer our fears about the unknowns ahead.

Any one of us who has ever faced a sleepless night of negative anticipation can identify with writer Shel Silverstein's poem *Whatif* (quoted in part):

> *Last night, while I lay thinking here,*
> *some Whatifs crawled inside my ear*
> *and pranced and partied all night long*
> *and sang their same old Whatif song:*
> *Whatif I'm dumb in school?*
> *Whatif they've closed the swimming pool?*
> *Whatif nobody likes me?*
> *Whatif a bolt of lightning strikes me?*
> *Everything seems well, and then*
> *the nighttime Whatifs strike again!*

What are the lyrics to your personal *Whatif* song? Your lyrics are those anticipated dilemmas and embarrassing events that likely aren't destined to happen.

In preparing to create a less stressful negotiation, review your lyrics and make a conscious decision about what is inconsequential and disposable and what is worth careful planning. *Whatifs* will disturb precious hours of sleep and cause havoc with daytime thoughts as well.

Do What You Do Best

Consider what you do that nobody else does as well before assigning responsibilities to yourself and others. What you do best is often what you enjoy most and what you have a natural talent for achieving.

Work with folks you trust. Don't be tempted with the *I might as well do it myself, since they'll only screw it up or not follow through.*

Amazing Grace

Singing *Amazing Grace* as a morning ritual gently warms up my voice, gives peace to my thoughts, and reminds me life is bigger than my next negotiation.

The phrase *When someone said I live in fantasyland, I almost fell off my unicorn* makes me smilingly remember not to take myself overly seriously. Your sense of humor is an essential business skill, serving to relax yourself, your team and your opponents.

The inner peace you develop for negotiating will carry through in every aspect of your life. You'll discover a peaceful self thinks more clearly, communicates more effectively and achieves goals more efficiently.

6 *Looking for Logic*

We think and reason to draw conclusions of truth. Logic is both a science and an art. Emotions and business intertwine. One negotiator's truth can differ substantially from another's.

Organized

My newspaper features editor is a fanatical organizer. Her favorite British *Punch magazine* cartoon shows a butler in an elegant living room, holding a vase with #7 on its base; a coffee table has a matching stenciled #7. Can we be logical without being organized? Can we be logical and organized without having a sense of humor? No on both counts.

I Think?

My philosophy professor's favorite cartoon shows a soul-searching fellow who inspires quests for logic with a six-word caption:
>*I think. Therefore I am. I THINK?*

We think and persevere in creatively researched, dynamically contemplated, impeccably detailed proposals. We need to be mindful of hubris: stubborn false pride makes us certain we're right when we're wrong.

Be gentle with ourselves: It's difficult to admit the seemingly logical path we've mapped has mine fields on the right, swamps to the left and a surprise cliff past those bushes.

Homes-Sweet-Homes

Likely your opponent is not seeking to puzzle or bewilder you with his logic, any more than you are trying to purposefully perplex him. Complications, uncertainty and confusion never add to a smooth negotiation.

A common human denominator is experience with home renovations. We, as logical negotiators, seek to take control. We research options from style advice to consumer quality and get recommendations for products and service providers. We think about our homes-sweet-homes getting homier and sweeter. We visualize results we can live with joyfully.

Negotiations essential to renewing our abodes fit perfectly into the looking-for-logic model. Persevering isn't always in our best interests. However, because we take our homes personally and involve our emotions, logic may quickly go out the windows. Our personal mindsets complicate perplexing matters when we disagree with contractors and tradesfolk.

Lost in Translation

We must confirm that we are speaking the same language. I'm not referring to being lost in translation. The words and phrases we us -- spoken and written --can easily be misunderstood. The only contract with more potential problems than oral agreements are those lacking specifics or including clauses subject to misinterpretation.

Does our contract specify a step-by-step timeframe for all aspects of the renovations? Is there a penalty clause if our contractor doesn't perform as promised? When our contractor's crew is knocking the place to bits at seven a.m., do we wander around the kitchen, pretending to be thankful they showed up at all?

It is essential to take the emotion out of our actions. Being civilized and polite ought not prevent us from communicating assertively to the contractor who signed on the bottom line.

We become dissatisfied with many aspects of the renovations. We rationalize about why not to cancel the contract and seek a more competent contractor. Our attempts to negotiate further with the contractor fail.

The phrase, "Good money after bad" has merit. Our personal lives and loved ones are more important than completing the guestroom in a haze of anger and bitterness. Letting go and starting over will provide a sense of we're-not-victims relief. We are logical negotiators who have learned from our experiences to negotiate more effectively next time.

Detailed Agenda

It's reasonable to think we logical negotiators are more business oriented than emotionally focused. We create detailed meeting agenda with timing for each speaker. The Q&A period precedes follow-up assignments with career consequences for nonperformance.

The logical negotiator, craving an on-target and productive meeting, may banish beverages, snacks and, by gosh, chairs from the room. A standing meeting of hungry and thirsty folks may not be good for morale, but accomplishes more in less time.

Control

When we are certain logic, perseverance and understanding of perplexing negotiations are under our control, we take action with faith in ourselves are logical negotiators. Take to heart my attorney's favorite cartoon, the classic *New Yorker* magazine's business executive responding to an appointment request, "Never. Is never good for you?"

7 *Opponents Who Frustrate*

Ah! Humankind's free will. Used for good and evil. Let's put those frustrating negotiators in the evil category and examine how best to deal with them.

Negotiating can be defined as attempting to achieve a mutually agreeable solution, often in a challenging situation. When we're faced with an opponent who lives to be self-important, easily angers and detests compromise, we are entitled to be frustrated.

Learning to control our thoughts, words and physical reactions when we feel frustrated can be a major achievement. We have a choice, either to transform ourselves into calm, composed, successful winners, or suffer as masochistic cynics with unachieved negotiating goals.

Looking Inward

Examine your own negotiating behaviors and you may be surprised to discover they replicate the most annoying behaviors you find in others. These are the behaviors that set off your hot buttons, even if you'd prefer not to admit it. No matter how difficult to do, swallowing your pride and admitting such negatives exist within you is essential.

Behavioral examples include, but aren't limited to: off-topic distractions; promises without follow-through; poor verbal and/or written communication skills; sarcasm; overreactions; making excuses; rejecting hard truths; and explosive anger.

Once you are self-aware, take time and energy to change each behavior for the better. You will discover these behaviors frustrate you less in yourself and in others. Only you can dig deep and examine your history to figure why you behave as you do and how change will benefit you.

Basics in Place

Preparing the basics necessary for every negotiation -- knowing your goals, doing your research, preparing your communications -- form your foundation for negotiating with frustrating people. When you are satisfied that your basics are in place, you can expand your negotiating expertise with these challenging opponents.

Before the Meeting

Before your initial negotiation meeting is scheduled, control as much as you possibly can by confirming details in writing as to time, place, agenda and participants. The mantra "A verbal contract is as good as the paper it isn't written on" is a good reminder of the importance of also not relying on phone conversations or voicemail messages.

A Positive Attitude

Start your face-to-face encounter with confident body language, a smile, a sturdy handshake, and eye contact. Use small talk judiciously to relax yourself and your opponent. Your research will provide information about him that you can use to show interest and optionally massage his ego.

Taking Control

When your opponent is behaving and talking in a manner that frustrates you:

Review the agenda together. Determine which topics are essential for the day's meeting. Agree on which topics to delay to another meeting. Do not waste time on non-essential topics that require lengthy discussion. Agree to disagree about them and remove them from the negotiation.

Deal with his angry outburst with calmness. A calm demeanor engenders clear thinking. Instead of encouraging his rage, it will motivate him to mirror your composure.

Remember that no response is a strong message in and of itself.

Know how much decision-making authority your opponent holds. Your opponent may claim that he must seek approval from a power-that-be above him. If you know full well that he is the final decision-maker, tell him so.

Use the meeting agenda to stay on topic. The moment your opponent tries to kidnap the conversation inappropriately, interrupt him and quickly return to the negotiation's focus.

Respond to irrationality with logic. Figure out why your opponent is being unreasonable and counter with your own information. Prioritize intellect over instincts.

Give everyone an old-fashioned time-out. Be clear how long the break will take.

Negotiating Limbo: When to Let Go

You have tried every sensible, logical and creative response. Despite your efforts, the negotiation is still going nowhere and has little hope of even arriving there. Decide how best to let go. Prepare and deliver your communications aloud and soon thereafter confirm your message in writing. Be crystal clear that you are unwilling to continue wasting your time and efforts.

Choosing to say it is over in a perpetually wait-wait instead of win-win negotiation is a decision to leave the frustrating confines of masochistic limbo.

As Albert Einstein wrote, "The world is a dangerous place to live; not because of the people who are evil, but because of the people who don't do anything about it."

8 Reinventing Yourself as a Negotiator

In the Beginning: Your Negotiating Style

Even if you consider Adam and Eve's story an apocryphal adventure, as a negotiator reinventing yourself you will reap the benefits of examining their Garden of Eden shenanigans.

Imagine yourself as one or more of the characters in Eden. Who does your personal negotiating style or styles emulate? Don't hold back -- you want to face the good and evil of the naked truth and put your thoughts in print.

God *Creative, innovative, all-knowing leader. Flexible to a point, over-reacts to anger issues.*
Adam *Proud, first of his kind, willing to share. Acts before thinking, doesn't consider consequences.*
Eve *Helpmate, curious, shares joys. Easily manipulated, blames others for own decisions.*
Serpent *Motivator, concise communicator. Troublemaker, liar, no concern for others.*

Tweeting about Your Skills and Talents

These are not tweets to share: They're purely to inform you about you. In a 140-character maximum tweet confession, non-censoring stream-of-consciousness, reveal the talents and abilities you're proud of, come naturally, work to your benefit easily and often.

In a second tweet, reveal those characteristics you find frustrating, ineffective, unprofessional.

Read both tweets several times, experiencing your emotional reactions as positives and negatives.

Applying Your Insights

Select a recently concluded negotiation and jot down a summary description. Choose a negotiation you think of as important, but that you're reliving all too often, wishing you could do over, second-guessing how your actions and attitude affected the outcome. You're about to do an in-depth examination of that negotiation. You don't have a word limit. You do have an obligation to yourself to remember that negotation in detail:

What were your goals?

Who were your allies and competitors?

What were your skills, talents, knowledge, experiences?

What was the outcome?

Your Answers Are Keys to Negotiating Effectively

Did you give into temptation, revealing your low figure before your competitor revealed his? Did you maximize the effectiveness of your verbal and written communications abilities? Did you over- or underreact to an emotional moment?

How much clear thinking did you do before responding? Were future consequences a consequential part of your thinking? Did you find it impossible to delay immediate gratification?

What else frustrated you in the planning stage, during and after the negotiation? If you had a chance to negotiate the same situation over again, what would you do differently? Of equal importance, what would you do the same or even moreso?

Did you let self doubts influence your negotiating? Was time management a factor in the negative results? How well did you research the negotiation topic and your competitors' resources and needs. Were you flexible with your personality traits to match those of your competitors?

Were you intimidated when your competitor played the 'I have to check with a higher authority' gambit? Did you allow yourself to be intimidated or distracted?

Your On-Camera Challenge

Jot down a summary description of the next important negotiation in your life.

You're about to communicate intimately with the most important person involved in your next negotiation: You.

Set up your video equipment. Protect yourself from interruptions.

Stretch. Sit comfortably. Turn the camera on, smile and record only positive thoughts about the purpose of the negotiation:

Reviewig the video, you will learn:

   To recognize and appreciate your talents and abilities;

   How to gain the respect and cooperation of your competitors;

   What personality traits are appropriate to communicate your ideas and goals, and

   Why a positive outcome is in your future.

Watch your video, not only to review your positive attributes, but also to realize how much you've changed through the confidence of self-knowledge as a negotiator.

Self-awareness is, after all, a positive aspect of our human condition wherever we create our lives outside the Garden of Eden.

9   Negotiating with Friends

So very often, we negotiate with folks who are our business associates, partners and colleagues, and who also have personal places in our lives. It's a tricky business that goes beyond the standard dynamics of negotiating into an intimate realm filled with dangers. Dangers include possibly losing a good friend, a business relationship, or both.

We humans have limitless potential to love and be loved. Practice our passions. Focus on our talents and leave legacies for future generations. Give from our hearts, minds and souls. Amaze and astonish by creating what never existed before. And Lord, all too often we royally screw it up: Let's examine how not to.

In the Beginning

You share a history with your college roommate, having become best friends as freshmen, you lived through the joys, trials and tribulations of transforming yourselves from inexperienced students to knowledgeable adults. In a moment of grand enthusiasm, you decide to create a business based on your mutual talents. What is, after all, the point of entrepreneurship that doesn't lead to career and personal success?

Negotiator, first: Friend, second

All the basic tenets of negotiating are even more essential when friends negotiate. As an example, I'll use college roommates/entrepreneurs.

Negotiator, first: Friend, second:

Establishing a new business requires negotiating beyond the logic of applying each person's attributes to achieving mutual goals in multiple roles. The advantages of knowing each other's personalities, experiences and quirks are outweighed by the realities of dueling egos.

"During a negotiation, it would be wise not to take anything personally. You will be able to see opportunities more objectively," wrote Brian Koslow, author of *Self-Made – Generate Wealth Like a Millionaire.*

Beyond titles: The math whiz who is providing 75% of initial funding is chief financial officer. The well-Linkedin extrovert is president; his connections encompass unlimited sources of professional expertise, prospective clients and potential employees. It is the honest discussion and specific, written delineation of job descriptions beyond top titles that will eliminate dueling egos.

Equally essential, is communicatively effectively to prove how each friend is assigned a percentage of the company's value. Motivational speaker Zig Zigler tells us, "Money isn't the most important thing in life, but it's reasonably close to oxygen on the 'gotta have it' scale."sa

Time is of the essence: We negotiators are fully aware of the importance of timing, presenting ourselves as focused professionals, bringing up topics at appropriate times, avoiding issues when stress and deadlines demand doing so.

Business partners who work and socialize together cannot underestimate the necessity for time apart. Absence can make the heart grow fonder and the business run smoother. It supplies not only physical separation and time to appreciate other aspects of the partners' individual lives. People maintaining dual roles as business associates and friends can, with privacy, personal advocations to distract, and commitment to thought, put an objective twist on negotiating for win-win results.

You Want Me to Do What?

Even when we know a business partner/friend very well, situations will arise that surprise us, not with delight, but with anger. Mastering these emotional moments differ from negotiations with people we will likely never encounter again. Even when we are not in the same room as our business partner, we may not be able to get them out of our thoughts.

Business partners do well when they agree to perpetually say what they mean and mean what they say. The *"You want me to do what?"* response, delivered lightly, smilingly, yet sincerely, will lighten your angry reaction and put your friend on immediate notice that he is asking for the impossible or unimaginable. It is then time to come full circle to rethinking and rephrasing the request and continuing a productive conversation between friends.

Knowing Too Much about Each Other

John D. Rockefeller, industrialist and philanthropist, warned, "A friendship founded on business is better than a business founded on friendship."

It is unfair, unbusinesslike and unprofessional to take personal knowledge into negotiations. It is also impossible not to do so. The key is thinking through to be fully aware of how and why you are using inside information is to influence the negotiation's outcome. Business will flourish when both cfo and president mindfully give priority to mutual benefits.

Daring Onward

In a world where we're multitaskers, becoming experts at simultaneously succeeding as business people and friends is still challenging. It is a challenge, however, so rich in personal and professional rewards that we must -- for ourselves and each other -- strive to negotiate as if our lives depended upon doing so: For they do.

10 Mantra: Time is Money; Money is Time

Einstein feverishly scribbles equations on a blackboard in Gary Larson's *The Far Side* cartoon. The caption reveals the answer to one of life's mysteries: Einstein discovers that time is actually money.

After our grins fade, we negotiators realize that phrase conveys a solid truth. Its counterpart is equally valid: Money is actually time.

Taking Time

Taking time is a positive mindset to seize the day with thoughtful respect for the power time has over our lives. It's the diametric opposite of lollygagging through life in idle thoughts and inconsequential activities.

Time you invest in preparing yourself and the specific details of your negotiation project goals is essential to success.

De-briefing yourself and your colleagues after winning is worth the time you'll spend together. It is the perfect way to recognize those aspects of the negotiation that you can use in future negotiations.

In a negotiation, taking time relates to how you decide to pace and control your communications. The patient, closed-mouth negotiator waits (despite uncomfortable silence) for his opponent to be the first to reveal financial terms. Be patient. Show little emotion and confident body language. Relax your demeanor.

Leeway

Pilots and ship captains define leeway as the amount a plane or vessel is blown or drifts off its normal course by crosswinds. Back on dry land, leeway means extra time, space and materials. For negotiators, leeway is a degree of freedom for action and thought.

Have you let leeway disappear from your life? Are you so tightly committed to a negotiation that a minor blip causes a quickened heartrate and necessitates last-minute changes in your well-honed plans?

Leeway provides breathing room and space -- excellent for mental health and clear, unpressured thinking. One effective leeway action is regularly scheduling time with and for yourself. For example, calendar your leeway meeting with yourself every Tuesday and Thursday from 9:00 to 9:30 a.m.

Overestimate the time necessary to achieve each step toward your negotiation goal and include that extra time for flexibility in your plans.

Perfectionism and Control

Ah, you are so good at doing so many things. Multitasking is part of your genetic makeup. But have you considered asking yourself, "Am I the best person for this job, or would my time be bettter focused on achieving something else?"

Two intertwining issues come to mind: Perfectionism and Control. Consider one step in a negotiation project near and dear to your heart:

Does it have to be done perfectly?
What are the consequences of a slightly imperfect result?
What are the time, energy and resources required in each case?
Assign a project to a staff member, even if your inner control freak fears she won't do it perfectly.

Stop Thinking: Start Doing

You think about what you have to do, then you don't do it, perhaps even praising yourself just for thinking. You spend time frustrated, worried, procrastinating. Whenever you spend more time thinking about a task than actually taking actions to accomplish that task, Stop Thinking: Start Doing. The more you do so, the more natural and easy doing so will become.

Money is Actually Time

You can invest in yourself by using your money to buy yourself time.

Upgrade technology as soon as it fits into the criteria of making you more efficient and effective. Give your personal or virtual assistant additional responsibilities that don't require your expertise or attention.

Invest in activities that better your mental, emotional and physical health. Thinking more clearly, communicating more effectively and having more energy are valuable in seizing the minutes, hours and days of your life.

Benjamin Franklin

Founding Father Benjamin Franklin played many roles, despite having the same 24 hours a day you and I do. He was a successful author, printer, political theorist, politician, postmaster, scientist, musician, inventor, satirist, civic activist, statesman, and diplomat. In his 1748 pamphlet *Advice to a Young Tradesman*, Franklin wrote, "Remember, time is money. Waste neither time nor money, but make the best use of both." His advice holds true for today's negotiators.

11   Intimate Negotiating

In the committed, close, personal relationships we regard as intimate, negotiating is perpetual. These are the people we know best and who know us best. We can improve our intimate negotiating skills and results by examining interactions between traditonal husband and wife duos and variations thereon. Couples who live, play and work together -- in a family business or entrepreneurial endeavor -- provide additional dynamics. These negotiating techniques provide positive results both personally and professionally.

Say What You Mean: Mean What You Say

In Brad Meltzer's *The Inner Circle* the author states, "There's nothing more intimate in life than simply being understood. And understanding some else."

Your skills as an intimate negotiator reach beyond the words you say and write. They reach into the heart of effective communications and to the fearful environs of whispering to hide the truth and screaming to get your points across. No one said it would be easy. If they had, they were wrong.

Communicating effectively means with each other, scheduled in advance as much as possible to avoid bad timing, bad moods and bad karma. It means taking advantage of those things you both naturally agree about. It also means thinking through individual skills, talents and preferences and sharing the wealth and frustrations of life's responsibilities. Not talking honestly leads to not making decisions, which leads to anger about priorities not getting done.

We respond as if we could read each other's minds. We answer questions before our beloved finishes asking them. In anger, we reveal intimate knowledge in public situations.

Declare Peace in the Battle of the Sexes

Be certain you and your partner discuss and agree about priorities that concern you both. Acknowledge the common points you both resonate positively about. Agree to disagree peacefully and go one step beyond: Don't reiterate how you wisely agree not to disagree. Focus on those things that provide mutual satisfaction.

Whether you consider yourself overworked or under-appreciated (or both), the idea of coming to terms about non-negotiable items as realities will brighten your lives. Identify items you consider non-negotiable. Come to terms on these items prior to proceeding with negotiable items. For example, your non-negotiable item is attending church every Sunday. Your spouse's is not being reminded that sports car he bought in a fit of mid-life crisis was a mistake. Non-negotiable items, once agreed upon, are not subjects of discussion or derision.

Don't fall for gender stereotypes. Women who ask questions want more than a patient listener; they want advice and solutions. Men are willing to share problems when women don't automatically change the topics to their own difficulties.

Cut the drama and the generalizations. Relationships will always have hot-button issues that wreak havoc with effective communications. The more important and complicated the issue, the more likely one or both negotiators will become dramatic, illogical and frightened.

Try the technique of breathing deeply, smiling, stretching and calming yourself in words, attitudes and physicalities. Declare a time-out if talk is just a maddening waste of time, but agree on how long that time-out will last. Be wary of saying 'you always,' and 'you never.'

The delicate nature of not wanting to hurt the other person's feelings requires active self-discipline. Sarcasm, accusations, over-reacting, changing topics, holding grudges, and unnecessarily bringing up the past into the present will only hurt everyone involved.

Timing

Timing is one of the most delicate matters between couples. Even larks (early risers) and owls (late preferers) can learn to live together. Differing body rhythms can be positive if used wisely, allowing for privacy and time for contemplation without interruptions. Vow to value your partner's time.

Be present and attentive to each other. Technology, albeit timesaving, can destroy intimacy. Compulsive connectivity ought not replace real-time conversations. Smile at each other over the breakfast table without staring down at your iPads.

Elizabeth Gilbert, *Committed: A Skeptic Makes Peace with Marriage* wrote, "Every intimacy carries secreted somewhere below its initial lovely surfaces, the ever-coiled makings of complete catastrophe." Yet every intimacy carries above its surfaces multiple opportunities to create loving, productive, fulfilling lives together."

12 Negotiating Isn't Child's Play

Birthrights

You were born with the ability to negotiate. Although negotiating isn't child's play in the sense of being purely easy and fun, the innate talents you used for your earliest communications will take you far in your adult negotiations. Free yourself from the series of acts inherent in the serious business of negotiating.

Consider the Time-Out

A misbehaving child is confined to a private spot to quietly think about her misbehavior. When the time-out times out, she exchanges an apology for a hug. The procedure has merit, even if the participants are midlife crisis, not pre-kindergation age. An hour break may be all both sides need to recoup and reconsider why their negotiation isn't flowing smoothly. Handshakes not hugs are recommended.

Win at Under-the-table Gamesmanship

As a volunteer elementary school reading teacher, I'm often faced with a group of four or five children who display differing aptitudes and attitudes toward learning to read. Inevitably, one of the youngsters cannot or will not resist disrupting and distracting the others. A six-year-old boy throws a pencil under the school library table and jumps down to retrieve it.

The ego-massage-questing executive expounds on topics unrelated to the negotiation. He may even pre-arrange interruptive phone calls requiring his immediate attention and expertise.

The negotiating key is making these insecure individuals the centers of attention before they misbehave. As soon as the tutoring group arrives, I tell the young man he is in charge of keeping his classmates well behaved.

As the meeting begins, praise the executive for his abilities to keep everyone focused on the matters under discussion.

Show...

When Evan, age nine, led me to the electronics department of a major chain store, he knew exactly what he wanted. 'It's educational," he announced, pointing to a multimedia contraption priced at $99. His face said it all: If you love me, dear godmom, you'll buy it for me. Keeping emotionality out of negotiations (although I do love him) is always best.

We power-walked across the megastore to the food department. I asked Evan to stand up straight and hold his arms out. He looked puzzled: Keeping your opponent puzzled is a good negotiating technique. As I reached into the food locker and took out box after box of his favorite school lunch (the kind that's fun to eat and holds more nutrition in the cardboard box than its contents), I convinced Evan to balance 30 boxes.

His eyes peered out from the array, questioning my purpose. 'Evan,' I explained, "those 30 days worth of lunch cost the same amount as this 'educational' toy.' " We restocked the lunches and power-walked back to electronics. Evan grinned as he chose a nine-dollar robot designed to hone his programming skills.

...and Tell

If a picture tells a thousand words, a site visit to the building you're negotiating to purchase will give both you and the owner a reality-based (instead of boardroom PowerPointed) look, feel and reaction to details. Getting out of the electronics department shown above or escaping from the official venue provides not just a physical change, but a head-clearing emotional one as well. Back in the boardroom, tell that other fellow what you saw has locked in your determination and provide the specifics about how the experience solidified your expectations.

Confuse Them With Kindness

Even a toddler will quickly learn that the more he asks, the more he can expect to receive. Adults play the numbers, too, in negotiations. At all ages, requesting items you don't really want or need in a long list of requests allows you to be the gentleperson, seeming to be cooperative and reasonable as you let the other person 'convince' you to give in, time after time.

Follow the toddler comfortably carted around the supermarket, loudly asking for whatever non-nutritious goody he passes; you'll recognize him at the checkout counter, when the dad who persistently turned him down finally buys him a bag of candy.

Consider the church choir director, who presents dozens of pieces of sheet music at the first rehearsal before Easter. Imagine the choir members' relief as they 'convince' her which hymns and anthems they can't possibly learn before the blessed season. Does she succeed thanks to her negotiating skills or is it a higher power looking after her? You decide.

13 Ego Massaging to Negotiate Positively

Being human, we want what we want when, where, why and how we want it. It's a life force we can't change, so I'm positive that controlling our attitudes and actions can only benefit each of us mentally, emotionally and physically. This control will bring about positive results in our roles as negotiators – before, during and after every negotiation.

Self-Indulgent Contemplation

Think about your first successful negotiation. Indulge in self-satisfactory memories: I certainly won't ask you to wipe that grin off your face. But I will encourage you to recall details of what you did and what part positive thoughts and actions contributed to your defining it as successful. Consider how it was successful not only for you and your team, but also for your opponent.

Massaging your ego (deservedly so), gets you ready to make negotiating positively the substance of your style. Your successful negotiation created the groundwork to build longterm relationships, improve communications and solidify win-win outcomes. Verbally massaging your opponent's ego will provide positive mutual benefits.

Combining the wisdom of experts with your experiences will transform you into a naturally positive negotiator.

Norman Vincent Peale: Pastor

In his perenially bestselling *The Power of Positive Thinking*, Norman Vincent Peale advises, "Formulate and stamp indelibly on your mind a mental picture of yourself as succeeding. Hold this picture tenaciously. Never permit it to fade. Your mind will seek to develop the picture. Do not build up obstacles in your imagination."

Expanding on Peale's positive visualizing:

When you create a mental image of your successful self, what do you look like, what are wearing, how confident is your demeanor and body image, how professional are the content and delivery of your communications? Be objective: Would you be impressed when you showed up to negotiate? What do you need to change about you to increase your confidence level?

Is your imagination running wild with non-existent obstacles? Are you focused on 'what-if' scenarios that are upsetting and confusing you? What if you thought about solutions to the 'what-ifs' before they happened? What if you calmly realized that they never will?

Herm Albright: Cynic and Humorist

Herm Albright, 19th century German painter and lithographer, said, "A positive attitude may not solve all your problems, but it will annoy enough people to make it worth the effort."

Self-confession: When folks inquire, "How are you?," I respond, "Annoyingly happy." I'm within my rights as a newlywed wife to evoke their smiles.

In the meeting room, what can you do to use a positive attitude to simultaneously annoy and amuse your colleagues and opponents? By taking control of how less-than-seriously you respond, you relax yourself and them.

Henry Ford, II: CEO, Family Business

"Never explain; never complain."

Do you talk too much, revealing details that aren't appropriate for the negotiation at hand, much less any of your opponent's business? Does telling it all make you feel more or less in control of the situation? Or are you providing explanations to put a positive spin on conveying your goals? If you responded yes to that last sentence, change Ford's phrase to "Sometimes explain," but only when it is essential.

Visualize yourself again, this time determinedly talking about what you and your opponent are doing and saying that will expedite the negotiation's successful conclusion. Is there a purpose in complaining about the room temperature, bad internet connections, your opponent arriving late? If you 'complain' briefly with a solution in mind, go for it. Otherwise, 'never complain' will prove useful in maintaining your positive negotiating style.

Cheshire Cat: Nemesis, 'Alice's Adventures in Wonderland'

Smile as you emulate Alice's Cheshire Cat by revealing a self-satisfied grin that says I'm in control of myself and what I want to happen, will happen. Truth be told, the Cheshire Cat was pretending, fully aware that life in Wonderland was a series of ridiculous challenges with absurd characters. Perhaps that's how you'd describe recent negotiations, so you can see how essential a strong sense of humor is to negotiating positively.

The Cheshire Cat had another positive power play. He disappeared slowly, at will, reappearing as he liked. Visualize yourself standing up and leaving the room, neither explaining why nor looking back. When you return, grin confidently.

The Buddha: Enlightened Spiritual Leader

"What we think, we become. All that we are arises with our thoughts. With our thoughts, we make the world." In our world filled with negotiations, The Buddha was truly enlightened.

14 Stylish Negotiator

"This above all: to thine own self be true.
And it must follow, as the night the day,
Thou canst not then be false to any man."

Polonius to his son Laertes
Shakespeare's Hamlet, Act 1, scene 3

Being true to yourself as a negotiator requires knowing what type of negotiator you are. By reviewing details about the four types -- organizer, free spirit, egotist and gentle soul -- you'll learn which styles of thinking, acting and reacting will prove most effective.

One negotiator type in particular may resonate in your heart and head. However, we negotiators change, adjust and respond depending on the negotiation itself. The topics and people involved will provide strong and varying impacts. It is essential that you ebb and flow as best to glide gently over any troubled waters they create.

The more you know about the other types, the better you'll be able to use their styles to your advantage. Whenever you deem it appropriate, borrow attributes from other types.

Organizer

John's motto is, "Everything is under control." And he really believes it is true. His plans are well researched and detailed.

He knows all the specifics about strategies and tactics to achieve his negotiating goals. He becomes sarcastic when his opponent mumbles, "The contract is around here someplace."

He believes every item ought to be in its place (folder, computer file, iPad synced to every other electronic device he owns and all backed up in the Cloud.) He is intimidating, but will lose that control to frustration when a minor item is amiss in print or in conversation.

You can take advantage of John when he's distracted by lack of perfection during the negotiation. That's the best time to be calm and bold, phrasing your own goal with assurance that it will complement and restore his organized position.

Free Spirit

Amelia can charm the birds from the trees. Her image -- smile, posture and wardrobe -- is welcoming. She presents herself as a confident executive who has perfected a Buddha-like calmness, although her exuberance and chatty nature are not Buddha correct.

She revels in all aspects of the negotating process, with in-person communications, body language and gentle hugs far outweighing formal preparations. Her major sense is humor.

Amelia has difficulty understanding opponents who are not free spirits like herself. You can take advantage by responding to her cheery persona with a smile and stating how your goals will benefit you both. It will delight her and move the negotiation forward.

Egotist

Charles is very important to Charles and, therefore, to his negotiating team and his opponents. He knows it all and quite a bit more. In his world, there are two ways of negotiating -- his way and the wrong way. He thinks his time is much more valuable than yours is.

Charles is a poster child for the Peter Principal, promoted to his level of incompetence in the corporate hierarchy. He doesn't ask permission before taking action; he only apologizes after if he deems doing so can't be avoided.

He loves to talk about himself and strives to be the center of attention. When Charles reveals more than you need to know about Charles, you can take advantage of opportunities to flatter him about his fascinating anecdotes. Then swiftly segue into a focus of the negotiation that will benefit you from his revelations.

Gentle Soul

Patricia was born to please, a trait that frankly is not a prime attribute in negotiating. She will naturally like you and expect you to like her. You may hesitate to negotiate with gusto and guile: Do not hesitate.

Patricia cherishes win-win negotiations from start to finish. She's ready to meet in the middle. Find the emotional middle of your relationship and you may get your fair share.

Be careful of her natural abilities to gain control. Patricia speaks so softly that you can hardly hear her. As you move closer, she creates a bond of intimacy. She will gently ply her requests before you realize what is happening. Take advantage by leaning back instead, forcing her to move toward you or speak loudly enough for the conversation to continue.

Loyalty to Yourself

Shakespearean scholars describe being true to one's own self as the perfect virtue for protecting your own image and interests. Whether you are an organizer, free spirit, egotist, gentle soul or a well-considered combination of these negotiator types, the Bard's blessing is self loyalty.

15 Blessed Body Language

Right Reverend Michael B. Curry
Bishop of the Episcopal Diocese of North Carolina

Bishop Curry's negotiating quest pervades every fiber of his being. The confidence he exudes is more than a blessing from heaven above. He is a negotiator with a mission: So are you.

Knowing Thyself

Negotiators with dynamic demeanors are more than the sum total of their appearance, facial expressions, posture, gestures, movements, eye contact and body rhythms. The ability to effectively communicate wordlessly can be neither contrived nor convoluted. It requires a determined and controlled predictability that takes its power from knowing thyself.

Let the Games Begin

Consider his grand entrance:

Bishop Curry, fully vested in his regalia, processes into the church and garners the rapt attention of every congregation member. He is garbed appropriately for his Sunday morning mission. His carefully planned sermon is a well focused communication of dynamic body language designed to convince his audience of the merits of his message and their part in devoting time to watch, consider and act.

Yes, I've just described the components of a negotiation, albeit without verbal components.

Consider your grand entrance:
Your appearance reflects an intimate knowledge of *GQ* or *Vogue*'s latest fashion recommendations, improved by your personal style. Or you are a 20-plus CEO of a high-tech company sporting a comfortable hoodie and jeans. Matters not. The point is that you are dressed as you deem essential to portray your impressive self.

Body in Motion

The drama of a body in motion ought not be underrated. Without benefit or encumbrance of written notes, the bishop moves up and down the church's center aisle, arms waving, hands strongly positioned, fingers pointing, as he mesmerizes his flock. His movements do not interfere with his spoken message, but serve to emphasis the most significant points.

You're seated at the head of the meeting room table, ready to greet folks coming into the room. Consider a standing greeting, a let's develop a sense of camaraderie before sitting down together to negotiate. How, how much and which parts of your person you deem appropriate for enhancing your communications are personal preferences. I recommend you do what comes naturally.

Traditional body language experts who generalize about particular positions, postures and movements offer clues into human interactions and reactions.

However, keep in mind that if you are uncomfortable forming a steeple with your fingers as a sign of thoughtful confidence, it will appear neither thoughtful nor confident. Arms crossed in defiance may simply be a negotiator with a chill trying to keep herself warm.

Face to Face

You have quirks: We all do. Let's recognize them in ourselves, and forgive and forget those that are not effective in negotiating.

Your demeanor may be stoic or smiling. Your eyes may twinkle with positivity, or your brows may form perpetual lines of thoughtfulness. Your natural inclination may be to cup your chin in your hand with your fingers on your cheek to demonstrate deep concentration. You may fidget to a fare-thee-well, twirling locks of hair, nibbling fingernails or giving yourself relaxing neckrubs -- all nervous habits or carefully planned distractions. You be the judge of what to keep, expand and avoid.

Three Commandments of Negotiating

Keep these commandments and your body language:

Honor thyself, thy team, thy opponents by keeping eye contact.

Thou shalt not steal, but instead give as many reasons as possible for your opponent to agree with your position. Use body language to show confidence in your message.

Thou shalt not covet, but negotiate to create a win-win outcome by controlling your own and paying attention to what your opponents reveal with their body language.

Final Note

Every Sunday, Bishop Curry is fully aware of the mission he is striving to accomplish and naturally applies his body language to communicate with his flock. Emulate him -- with the body language that comes naturally to you -- for negotiating success.

And no matter how well prepared you are for your negotiation, consider saying a little prayer.

16 *Negotiating for Life*

Negotiate as if your life depends on it: Because it does.

You may consider yourself a born negotiator, blessed with innate skills, talents and mindset for success. Or you may be facing the reality that learning more about the negotiating process, and taking time and energy for training, practice and experiences, will greatly improve your win-win rates.

In either instance, take to heart, mind and action the insight that since you negotiate every day of your life, it is logical and vital to do it to the best of your abilities.

Negotiating through Life

Negotiating with youself first is your lifelong responsibility. A fulfilling life is composed of making decisions, setting priorities, researching, planning, communicating, empathizing, and acting to achieve your goals -- all essentials of successful negotiating.

By thinking about your own personal and professional experiences, you will discover interesting revelations about and for yourself. These are revelations you can apply to future negotiations. I present my three examples of negotiating situations, asking you to identify, learn from, and resonate with them.

Negotiating with a Seven-Year-Old

Children are naturals at finding and sharing humor. Since I consider a sense of humor one of the more important senses in negotiating, I'm sharing a memory of interacting with the younger set to put life into perspective, relax and renew myself. It lessens my stress levels, while increasing my ability to concentrate.

My then seven-year-old godson Evan was determined to spend the afternoon boogie-boarding and swimming. The waves were too dangerous, the water too cold, so I negotiated a safe compromise that would satisfy him.

We ran across the North Carolina beach, slowing down only to admire the baby sandpipers learning to take wing, we played *What super power do you wish for?* He stopped, caught his breath, and proudly announced, "I wish I could fly and help the birds who were having trouble staying up in the air. I'd swoop under them and lift them up with both hands."

We revived our run, until I stopped to tell Evan, "I'd wish for the super power of making children happy." Evan responded, staring into my eyes, saying, "You can't wish for that: You already have it." Ten years later and writing this still makes me cry happy tears.

Funny Busines of Business

As Dabagian's artist representative, I negotiated contracts for books, greetings cards, calendars, advertising materials, and decorative accessories -- cookie jars to smartphone covers.

I dealt with business details, client meetings, and marketing plans. He invested time, talent and energy to create colorfully imaginative cartoons and caricatures to illustrate the products.

Division of labors of love best describes our relationship. I enjoyed using my negotiating talents to research prospective clients, come up with product ideas, approach and communicate with major corporations, and polish the nitty-gritty details of contracts. I also protected my artist from mind-changing demands for multiple revisions and emergency early deadlines.

Our first contract together was a worldwide success. Millions of his cartoon illustrations flooded the market and evoked smiles from product purchasers. I negotiated the artist's visit to meet with the executive vice president of sales at 3M Corporate Headquarters in St. Paul, Minnesota. They played golf and bonded at the 19th hole.

The artist and I were delighted with the royalty checks -- for the first cartoon-embellished Post-it® Notes.

Negotiating for a 90-Year-Old

My beloved Dad led a fullfilling and productive life. A World War II vet, he was a proud man of few words and much love.

Negotiating takes on a uniqueness of emotionalism when a daughter is taking care of her father's last few months on earth, determined to make him as comfortable and content as possible. The process was intimate and personal. It required the in-depth research, planning, logic, and communication skills of other negotiations.

Decision-making about his medical care, hospice and final plans necessitated communicating persuasively with healthcare professionals, hospital billing bureaucrats, and insurance companies.

The issues of giving up privacy and taking many medications required heartfelt energy to negotiate with the man himself, a man whose lifelong motto was *Everything's Under Control.*

Lifetimes

Our negotiations in life range from the sublime to the ridiculous. From birth to death, with all the amazing challenges and opportunities, celebrations and disasters, relationships and realities. Our negotiations -- large and small, personal and professional, complex and simple -- give us the power, obligation and challenge to improve our own lives and the lives of others.

The confident negotiator is always ready to negotiate for life.

17 Scarlett O'Hara Goes with the Win

Southern belle Scarlett O'Hara, heroine of Margaret Mitchell's *Gone with the Wind*, was portrayed with an independent attitude, an adventurous spirit, and an intriguing intensity toward getting her way.

From the beginning of the Civil War (1861-1865) until the end of the Reconstruction Era (1865-1877), Scarlett transformed herself from petulant manipulator to mature woman negotiator. Romance, history and techniques for negotiating life with intelligence and intuition abound in this Pulitzer Prize-winning novel of unrequited love and Southern survival.

Meet Scarlett and the men who shaped her talents and creativity as a negotiator.

Set Priorities

"Land is the only thing in the world that amounts to anything, for 'tis the only thing in this world that lasts."
Gerald O'Hara, Tara Plantation Owner, Scarlett's Father

Giving parental advice to 16-year-old Scarlett in 1861 wasn't any easier or immediately effective than it would be with a 21st-century teen. Teens of any era will roll their eyes, sigh deeply as adults share wisdom, and seek distractions – be it a getaway walk under the magnolias or a session tweeting.

Gerald O'Hara's daughter was caught in a love triangle with heart-throb Ashley Wilkes and her competitor Melanie Hamilton. Dad was attempting to comfort her as she faced the disappointment of the other woman winning her beloved beau.

Did her father's words, "Land is the only thing in the world that amounts to anything, for 'tis the only thing in this world that lasts," quickly convince Scarlett that the land is and will always be the most important thing in her life?

Is it worth the investment in time, energy and communication to propose lifelong values, as her father did? Yes, all y'all! By the end of the book, Scarlett learns that interpersonal relationships (including three marriages) diminish and disappear. Her decision to go home to Tara provides her comfort, hope and plans for the future.

Negotiating requires maturity. Ground yourself in what is truly important for the present and future. Consider your opponent's individual needs and behaviors and phrase your communications to direct his attention and actions.

Deliver your messages with confidence. Do not necessarily expect immediate positive results. Timing and patience are two attributes of excellent negotiators.

Think Courageously

*"The people who have brains and courage come through
and the ones who haven't are winnowed out."*
Ashley Wilkes, Southern Gentleman,
Scarlett's Unrequited Lover

Positive self-talk is the ability to convince ourselves that we can conquer challenges, change minds, and achieve the thought-of-as-unachievable. The successful negotiator is proud, confident and willing to take chances. She does all in her power to win.

Scarlett is a woman blessed with brains and courage. Her survival instincts control her behavior. As the Old South becomes history and Reconstruction creates the New South, she lets go of a past that is 'gone with the wind' of change. She cherishes historic values and acts upon those to benefit her future.

She comes to understand that having a flirty smile and a 24"-inch waist can't charm her way into business success. Learning to respect herself as a logical, determined and focused owner of, first a sawmill, then the plantation, requires her to become the self she was destined to be. Living in the present, Scarlett controls as much as possible of her future. How will you maximize your control over your future?

Give a Damn

"Rhett, if you go, where shall I go? What shall I do?"
Scarlett's plea to Rhett Butler
"My dear, I don't give a damn."
Rhett's response

Scarlett and Rhett are perpetually seducing each other. They live in a love-hate relationship based on their personality similarities and differences. They conquer life-threatening situations as they weave in and out of each other's lives. Rhett guides her safely out of Atlanta as the Northern forces burn the city to the ground.

He abandons her to join the Confederate Army before they reach Tara. This forces, then encourages, her to become her own woman, the woman who declared, "As God is my witness, I'll never be hungry again."

Who is your mentor, motivator and muse? As a negotiator, do your personal and professional support systems say what they mean and mean what they say? Do they offer honest and true reactions and opinions during negotiations? Are you a mentor, motivator and muse to someone else?

Think Ahead

"Tomorrow is Another Day."
Scarlett O'Hara

Consider Scarlett's insight: "I'll think of it all tomorrow, at Tara. I can stand it then. Tomorrow, I'll think of some way to get him back. After all, tomorrow is another day."

Even the best negotiators need the rest and restoration in thought and body supplied by a good night's sleep. When our challenges are overwhelming, rather than act abruptly and unclearly, remember that tomorrow is another day.

Be ready for a fresh start. Give yourself time to release the emotional components inherent in communications. Life is filled with ever-changing challenges and options. So are negotiations. Do you have the courage to examine your thoughts and deeds, to determine your wants and goals, before entering a negotiation?

The Best Way to Succeed Tomorrow
is to Plan for Today.

The prospect of change can put fear in our hearts and minds. Negotiating well is about controlling as much as possible of the situation. Scarlett's survival and her protection of family and friends meant being ruthless and taking ends-justifying-means actions.

Do you play according to society's rules? Scarlett's behavior caused her hardship and disappointment, even as she persevered. She stole her sister's fiance for money, not love. She killed a Yankee soldier to protect her kin at Tara. She pursued business issues soon after her daughter died in an accident.

70 NEGOTIATING FOR LIFE

We are not heroines and heroes of an historic novel. We are people negotiating our way through our lives with our own challenges. Learning to put our best selves forward (for we have to live with ourselves) is a page to be taken from our own life stories.

18 Humor and Negotiating

What do billionaire investor Warren Buffet, country music legend Kenny Rogers, and Pulitzer Prize-winning columnist Dave Barry have in common as negotiators? A sense of humor. You can learn from their penchants to make fools of themselves in public, play the game of life lightly but wisely, and exaggerate to a fare-thee-well.

Warren Buffett's Playful Side

Business students who score invites to Berkshire Hathaway's headquarters in Omaha spend a privileged day with the mentoring man himself, corporate chairman Warren Buffett. As they tour local Berkshire-owned businesses and share lunch at Buffett's favorite fast food hang-out, he provides a wealth of information, answering their investment, education and career questions.

The world's second richest man's negotiating success has a strong foundation in humor. He goes on to share such nitty gritty life lessons as:

- "It's only when the tide goes out that you learn who's been swimming naked" (consider Enron's aftermath)
- "No matter how great the talent or efforts, some things just take time. You can't produce a baby in one month by getting nine women pregnant."
- "Why not invest your assets in the companies you really like? As actress Mae West said, 'Too much of a good thing can be wonderful.'"

The insightful day ends with a photo shoot, each student choosing one serious and one funny pose. That's why a charmingly grinning Buffett and the students garner "Wall Street Journal" slide show coverage as they sport fuzzy red reindeer antlers. He gets down on one knee to propose to a much younger woman. Then he imitates the wide-mouthed silent scream from the movie "Home Alone."

Kenny Rogers' Gambler's Advice for Life

Gambling is, after all, a fascinating form of negotiating. I dare you to read these lyrics from Kenny Rogers' "The Gambler" without singing aloud and without realizing how much his advice applies to your non-Vegas negotiations.

> You've got to know when to hold 'em
> Know when to fold 'em
> Know when to walk away
> Know when to run
> You never count your money
> When you're sittin' at the table
> There'll be time enough for countin'
> When the dealin's done.

Negotiating has an inherent stress component. We take ourselves very seriously. Humor balances by relieving tension, enlivening communication and enhancing creativity. This chorus from "The Gambler" is a focused reminder to do our research and be well prepared. Feel that inner strength of self-confidence in making decisions and taking actions. Trust our intuition. Be patient, but know when time's up and time to move on is now.

Dave Barry Running for President

Humor columnist Dave Barry is a master of exaggeration. In his bestselling "Money Secrets," he divulges "An absolutely foolproof system for making money in the stock market, requiring only a little effort and access to time travel."

One of my prized possessions was the result of a negotiation with the man himself. Dave ran for President of the United States with the campaign slogan "It's Time We Demanded Less."

Dave was the nation's most successful syndicated columnist; I was penning columns for a local paper in North Carolina. We met at the National Society of Newspaper Columnists convention, where I tried to convince (negotiate with) him to let me write his column while he travelled the country gathering votes.

Did I exaggerate my humor writing skills and readership? Of course. Did he give me his column and go stumping around the country? No, on both counts. But I do have a photo with Dave and a scribbled note: JB - You can be on the Supreme Court. (Autographed, of course.)

Humor, Starring You

Seriously (okay, not so seriously) consider approaching your next negotiation by lightening up the content, demeanor and deliver of the conversation.

NEGOTIATING FOR LIFE

You needn't be a professional comedian. Truth be told, telling jokes is an art requiring talent and timing. Sharing personal anecdotes appropriate for the situation can bring the sides together if your story encourages participants to smile as they identify with your adventures.

19   Churchill's Bathtub

From the perfectly heated waters of a footed Victorian bathtub, the British Prime Minister led the Allies to victory in World War II. Sir Winston Leonard Spencer-Churchill, intellectual and wit, wordsmith and exhibitionist, dictated his strategies to Patrick Kinna, his wartime secretary. Kinna even spoke of the world leader as his "nude chieftain."

*"No idea is so outlandish
that it should not be considered
with a searching and steady eye."*

It was in his long and twice-a-day baths that Churchill crafted many of his strategies to defeat the Nazi onslaught, prepared his brilliant quips and created his negotiating plans that won the day with Allied leaders as diverse as Joseph Stalin, Franklin D. Roosevelt, and Charles DeGaulle. Unquestionably, he was one of the most successful negotiators of the Twentieth Century.

What made him so successful?

First, of course, was the time he spent meticulously planning his approaches to saving his nation, the vast British Empire, and the many defeated nations of Western Europe.

It was in the control and relaxation of his tub that he created plans to trade naval bases for destroyers with a neutral United States, encourage and ally with his old enemy the Soviet Union, and inspire his country to fight on despite the costs.

Buttressed by his planning and his certainty in goals, Churchill's negotiating successes were also marked by his adherence to several clear qualities:

"For myself I am an optimist.
It does not seem to be much use being anything else."

The first phase of negotiating like Churchill is being a self-centered optimist. Where, when and how do you do your best thinking? Churchill realized his relaxed body led quickly to clear thoughts.

His twice daily baths were a tradition (complete with cigar and tumbler of brandy), with members of the military and politics often in the room with him. If you usually picture Churchill nattily garbed in a suit, tie and hat, think towel instead.

"True genius resides in the capacity for evaluation
of uncertain, hazardous, and conflicting information."

Truly a man of words -- spoken and written -- Churchill was awarded the Nobel Prize in Literature in 1953 for his body of work, including a four-volume history of World War I, a six-volume memoir, and the speeches he delivered with such power and mastery.

Churchill's abilities to evaluate information and transform knowledge into motivating words were unsurpassed. His selection of short, Anglo-Saxon words, similes and metaphors, were often phrased with the beautiful simplicity of a Shakespearean sonnet.

On March 5, 1946, in Salem, Illinois, he mobilized America into action by intoning, "From Stettin in the Baltic to Trieste in the Adriatic an *Iron Curtain* has descended across the continent."

He mesmerized audiences with an unsurpassed style of vocal delivery and direct eye contact that made each individual feel as if Churchill was speaking directly to him.

His final drafts were formatted for ease in scanning the text, short phrases on individual lines (as a poet would), boldfaced points of emphasis, and expansive white spaces to mark long pauses.

As you prepare to negotiate, your true genius depends on taking the time, energy and effort to evaluate your information, to consider the validity of your sources and to focus on priorities. Find out as much as possible about your opponents' 'uncertain, hazardous, and conflicting information.'

"Courage is what it takes to stand up and speak."

Maintain the courage of your convictions. Those beliefs and opinions you hold firmly will motivate you to stand up and speak with confidence, elegance and purpose.

Churchill's intelligence, creativity, perseverance and limitless energy produced the courageous ideas he put into actions.

On May 13, 1940, in his first speech before the House of Commons of the Parliament of the United Kingdom, he said, "I have nothing to offer but blood, toil, tears and sweat. We have before us many long months of struggle and of suffering. You ask, what is our aim? I can answer in one word: Victory. Victory at all costs."

"Courage is also what it takes to sit down and listen."

Studying Churchill's speeches is certainly an excellent way to improve one's own performance. On October 29, 1941, Churchill delivered a speech to the students at Harrow School, his alma mater in north-west London.

The speech is remembered and recognized for a single line, "Never, never, in nothing great or small, large or petty, never give in except to convictions of honour and good sense."

When you stand up to speak in a negotiation, pinpoint your aim with clarity and specificity. With the conviction of your courage, (to coin a phrase), convince your opponent to accept your goal as his own.

Then, have the courage to know (as tempting as it may be to linger longer as the center of attention), to sit down and listen.

"One million pounds"

By verbally exploring what he values most, you will be better able to handle the financial aspects of the negotiation.

Consider this anecdote: At a dinner party, an inebriated Churchill asked a beautiful woman if she would sleep with him for one million pounds. "Perhaps," the woman replied." Churchill then asked, "Would you sleep with me for one pound?"

"Of course not, what kind of woman do you think I am?" the woman responded indignantly. "Madam, we've already established what kind of woman you are," said Churchill, "now we're just negotiating the price."

"You make a living by what you get.
You make a life by what you give."

Take Churchill's words to heart. His noble causes may outshine yours as a negotiator, but the message he delivered in Dundee, Scotland, on October 10, 1908, still rings true.

"What is the use of living, if it be not to strive for noble causes and to make this muddled world a better place for those who will live in it after we are gone?

"How else can we put ourselves in harmonious relation with the great verities and consolations of the infinite and the eternal? And I avow my faith that we are marching towards better days. Humanity will not be cast down."

"We are going on swinging bravely forward along the grand high road and already behind the distant mountains is the promise of the sun."

20 *Negotiating with Energy Vampires*

Dracula himself would be no competition for energy
vampires, those mortals whose purpose in life is to frustrate,
distract, depress and anger their opponents, colleagues,
friends and family. You have been bitten, albeit figuratively,
whenever you've attempted to negotiate with them.

The Count could, of course, fly off toward the full moon.
You're stuck with trying to make sense of a negotiation that
sucks the emotional, mental and intellectual life out of you.
The result is physically tiring to a fare-thee-well.

Playing the Game

You can win when you learn to play their game, your way.
The actions I'm recommending will stand you in good stead
in professional and personal negotiations. Your purpose is to
consider your own best self-interests while guiding and
motivating energy vampires to join you in communicating
logically and positively.

Accentuating the positive drives energy vampires crazy. It
plays against their natural tendencies toward self-pity and
complaining. However, flattery is a virtue when you are able
to strike just the right chord in complimenting them. It's
worth the research to discover their soft spots.

Strategies & Egos

My goal is to prevent your saintly patience from erupting
into thumping heartbeats and temptations to scream.

Energy vampires' strategies, actions and behaviors are as deceptively simple as they are maddening. The traditional win-win negotiation mindset never occurs to them. All aspects of the negotiation will revolve around an ego-focused what's-in-it-for-them philosophy.

Enabling

The more you enable energy vampires to take advantage of you, the more you will turn your frustration inwardly as anger. Only when you do not do their work can you stop this dastardly cycle of failing to set boundaries, pretending their problems don't exist, and providing money and other resources that allow them to continue on their illgotten paths.

Be specific in describing precisely what you want and when you want it. Energy vampires will interpret your requests as they like, not with accuracy or logic.

Everything in Writing

Energy vampires' memories and commitments to accuracy leave much to be desired. Early, email the agenda and materials requiring review. Include spokespeople and topics with specific start and end times. Bold face an RSVP request and follow up until you receive one.

Timing

You enter the meeting room confident and fully prepared. You expect the other side to be just as ready. They are not. Nor did they even intend to be.

Punctuality is anathema to energy vampires. Insecure and doubting their own powers, their strategy is to arrive late, keep you waiting and waste time blaming others for their delay.

A meeting that does not begin as scheduled punishes professionalism and rewards energy vampirism. Common sense, logic and respect for yourself and other on-time members of both negotiating teams necessitates adhering to agenda timing. It does not require summarizing what has occurred when the energy vampires finally arrive.

Mutual Goals

The goal of most negotiations is effective communications and compromise leading to both sides feeling like winners. The goal of energy vampires is based on denial, lying, procrastination and delusional thinking. They will often agree for the sake of getting items past the stage of discussion, while never intending to follow through on commitments.

Centering Attention

Communicating to energy vampires means being the center of attention. It is in your best interest to control how centering that attention can progress the negotiation.

Consider the Pareto 80/20 Rule that 80% of accomplishments are the result of 20% of actions. Focus attention of only those areas in which energy vampires hold both responsibility and authority for decision-making.

For the Record

A precise, careful, accurate written record of negotiation proceedings in essential. Audio or video recordings can be worth than weight in gold when memories reveal diametrically opposite realities.

Energy vampires are never anxious to do work, much less what they consider extra work. When you take the responsibility for the record of the proceedings, you know it will not only get done, but it will also reflect what took place.

No Decision is a Decision

Energy vampires refuse to face the reality that not making a decision is a decision. Give them only two choices or they will impede progress by using the *Yes, but…this is why it can't happen* gambit. You can agree to disagree and drop the non-essential topics forever. Essential topics need to be clearly and as concisely as possible negotiated within set timeframes.

They live to never do anything once if they can do it two or three times and still get nothing done. It is up to you to quickly stop the cycle. If the energy vampires' focus is on activity that is not destined to come to fruition, do not allow him to luxuriate in repetition.

Historical Count Dracula

I assure you that Transylvanian noble Vlad the Impaler (aka Count Dracula) never permitted himself to be bested in negotiations with energy vampires: Nor should you

21   Lincoln's Hat: Presidential Confidence

Tall fellow, sporting a Mad Hatter chapeau and a gentler-than-Mona Lisa smile, stands on the White House steps. Requesting a favor is both a popular sport and a serious business for the citizens seeking Abraham Lincoln's wisdom, kindness and power.

He tips his hat, turns and walks inside, where he meets with a fortunate few in his office. (For you budding history buffs, there was no Oval Office; the 16th President's office is now designated the Lincoln Bedroom.)

Think of yourself as among the chosen, trying to convince Lincoln that your cause is worth his time and attention. What favor do you seek? How will you prepare to convince him to grant your request? Are you at the ready to negotiate confidently with him? What will you learn from the encounter to broaden your 21st century negotiating success?

Lincoln's Hat

Shortly after Lincoln was inaugurated in March 1861, he and his cabinet members were given leather portfolios embossed with their names in gold leaf lettering. A man who perfected his own image, his black stovepipe hat was taller than those commonly worn, with the brim flattened to enhance his 6'4" height. Unlike the fancy briefcase, Lincoln explained it was the perfect place to carry about important papers while leaving his hands free to gesture.

*"Always bear in mind that your own resolution to succeed
is more important than any other."*
Abraham Lincoln

Lincoln lived long before the term *branding* would be applied
to creating personal and business identities. He was a 19th
century example of success in applying and publicizing his
expertise, abilities and competencies to differentiate himself
from other politicians.

He epitomized self-confidence in appearance and manner,
written and spoken word, and professional relationships.

Resolve to create your brand in three steps. Know what you
stand for. Focus on what makes you stand out. Market
yourself to advance your career.

*"Better to remain silent and be thought a fool than to speak
out and remove all doubt."*

The quiet part of negotiating successfully is often underrated:

Do your research.
Organize your thoughts.
Clarify your goals.
Roleplay your conversations with colleagues.
Practice your presentations.
By so doing, you will be in the enviable position of knowing
what to say and how to say it.

Of equal importance is knowing when to remain silent. Your silence will often give you control of your own behavior, helping to avoid missteps and misunderstandings. Silence forces your opponent to wait on your terms, increasing your command and lessening his self-confidence.

"You can fool all the people some of the time, and some of the people all the time,
but you cannot fool all the people all the time."

Steven B. Wiley, president and founder of the The Lincoln Leadership Institute at Gettysburg, is a renowned authority on Lincoln. He shared these essential points about Lincoln as a negotiator who knew how to treat people without foolishness.

Be authentic and concise.
Keep your principles.
Know your audience. Don't talk over their heads.
Rejuvenate a conversation with anecdotes,
   true or created for the occasion.
Use humor and storytelling to heal.

"Discourage litigation.
Persuade your neighbors to compromise whenever you can.
As a peacemaker,
the lawyer has superior opportunity of being a good man."

We negotiators have our own opportunities to be motivators, peacemakers and good people. Lincoln's legacy will always have historic importance we ordinary mortals never imagine achieving. We do, however, hold the power of acting on our own attitudes and ambitions in our negotiations.

"When I am getting ready to reason with a man, I spend one-third of my time thinking about myself and what I am going to say and two-thirds about him and what he is going to say,"
Abraham Lincoln

Negotiate, thoughtfully!

22 Negotiator Whisperer: Ranch Secrets

Folks in Any and all resemblances between calves, cows, heifers, bulls (the herd) and human negotiators (humans) is fully intentional and show no disrespect toward either group.

Positively Bullish Negotiating

The two thousand pound bull in our backyard pasture knows me and I know him, by appearance, attitude, movement, voice and our historical relationship. Ninety-one-ten was just a year old when, among all the bulls on the supplier's ranch, he quickly established eye-contact with me. I've learned during my ranching life, that the more you know about a bull or a bullish negotiating opponent, the more you can impress him by communicating effectively and the better the negotiation's outcome.

Please the Guy with the Power

Our single bull is responsible for performing his manly best with 28 cows and ten heifers (the latter aren't officially cows until they give birth). The future of our herd depends on his ability to negotiate with each female in heat to convince her that he's her guy. His macho appearance and demeanor, self-confident attitude and worldly-wise experience (this isn't his first year on duty) do the trick.

The more you know about the real decision-maker in a negotiation, the stronger your plan will be.

Are you dealing with the executives who, in spite of their acting macho, self-confident and experienced, nonetheless must appeal to a higher authority for final deal approval?

Do your criteria for a successful negotiation reflect the needs and wants held by your opponent's powerful guy? Do you know and use your strengths and abilities to the fullest effect? What do you offer that no one else does?

The Grass is Always Greener

We negotiators share 'the grass is always greener' mindsets with the bovine set. The herd does so literally, hearing our truck approaching the gate between pastures, they're enthusiastic, positioned to run into the next grassy expanse.

We humans all too often want the newest model, the next great version, the never-seen-before invention. In both cases, they and we might very well be better off in familiar territory, concentrating on enjoying nutritious greenery or accomplishing our work with technology we already know how to use.

Body Language

Body language for both two and four legged creatures refers to non-verbal messages we communicate in movements, gestures, vocal tones and facial expressions. Working as a cow whisperer, I've learned to respect our cows' 300-degree panoramic vision and ability to hear different sounds in each ear. When I come too close, loudly or quickly, the cows consider their 'flight zone' invaded and quickly communicate to me in body language by running away across the pasture

Human body language is our wordless way to gain control of a negotiation. From the moment you enter the meeting room and scan your opponents' faces, maintain a confident negotiator's posture and poise. Listen and watch interactions of your team and your opponents' team.

A sturdy handshake, sitting up straight but comfortably in your chair, forming a steeple with your fingertips before you speak, add to your authority. Like our bull, present a large presence, maintain eye contact, avoid inappropriate smiles, move and gesture slowly and deliberately.

Focus Like a Calf

Human negotiators need detailed plans about goals, resources and actions. We are highly distractable and sensitive to unintended insults and mispoken remarks. Mistaken pride in our productiveness as multitaskers wastes time and energy.

Within 30 minutes of their births, I've witnessed calves stand up, curiously view their new environs, walk over to their moms, and know how to nurse for sustenance. Newborns and the entire herd are great examples of focusing on what they need to achieve. They cooperate with family and friends and learn about life by imitating older cows' behavior.

Calves seek out the best sources of nutrition and protect themselves from the hot sun by gathering under creekside shaded trees. They pay attention to humans who come to make certain that they're healthy and, yes, contented.

Who can you, my human friend, rely on for wisdom? Seek an experienced negotiator wiling to share his expertise. What are you doing that hurts rather than helps achieve your goals? Are you being self-protective of your health, energy, resources and time?

Whisperers

Cow and negotiator whisperers have much in common. We're always cognizant of instincts, behavior and environment, whether in the pasture or the boardroom.

23 *Womanly Art of Negotiating*

Relaxing into the workday, I'm sipping tea from a mug emblazoned: Let Me DROP EVERYTHING and work on YOUR PROJECT. The tea soothes my throat and voice for today's meetings and caffeinates my body rhythms.

But it is the inspiring mug slogan that gives me a mental boost and a memorable reminder toward getting my way in today's negotiations. It does provide a tinge of cynicism. I suspect not everyone I deal with is sincere, truthful and seeking win-win results as much as I strive to be and do.

Cynicism, I tell myself, is not sinful. It's a proper balance, albeit often underutilized, for the sugar, spice and everything nice description of what little girls are made of. I'm firmly convinced from talking with women of various ages and experiences that this 19th century nursery rhyme theme is still part of female upbringing.

Change of Mindsets

We women don't give ourselves sufficient credit for the skills and experience, talents and intuition, that bring us personal and professional success in negotiations. Women wonder why. I suspect men wonder too.

In business, especially in negotiating, it's time to let go of those nursery rhyme and fairy tale messages. Let us replace being women in distress to being women in charge. Keep in mind that the basic tenets of win-win negotiations do not differ between the sexes.

It's our womanly mindsets of wanting to please, feeling less than confident, and communicating without strength that require improvement. We can persuasively and permanently change how we think, speak and act in negotiating situations.

Role Models

Which women come to mind when you think about successful negotiators? Do you think of their physical appearance first, or admire their negotiating abilities as savvy, intelligent leaders? Visualize Cleopatra, Queen of the Nile and US Secretary of State Hillary Clinton. Each, in her own way and in her own time, negotiates effectively, garners respect, and changes her world.

Develop your style and maintain your image with class, grace and consistency. Picture yourself as a powerful negotiator at a meeting on your schedule. You are maintaining a confident attitude because you've done all the research, and rehearsed and roleplayed your messages.

You are taking action on specific steps to accomplish your goals. Your words are precise and get directly to your point. Your declarative sentences never end with a nervous, up-pitched question mark. You don't add 'perhaps, maybe, or I wonder if' thus lessening your responsibility.

Reinvent yourself with a deep level of security.

Be the woman who asks for what you want and wants what you ask for. Don't allow that doubting little girl voice in your head to distract you. Don't allow your negotiating opponents to tempt you to drift off topic with words that insincerely flatter or evoke fear.

Mind Your Business: Business Your Mind

Pay attention to your woman's intuition. Don't sabotage yourself in negotiations by disregarding these basics:

Say less. Mean more. Don't volunteer information.
Maintain eye contact.
Smile like Mona Lisa. Make them wait for your response.
Don't fuss, fiddle or check your makeup.
Remember youand your opponent can't read each other's mind.
Invest in e-vices to enhance your effectiveness.

Two Women: Two Negotiating Styles

Learning by watching and listening to other women negotiate is empowering.

Angela's attitude is pure self-confidence. She never doubts that her way is the right way. Her communication style is brief, focused and specific. Her negotiating opponents immediately know her goal. She works the room, is the center of attention, and doesn't apologize for thinking others must prioritize her plan and goals.

Martha's eyes pierce right through you. She is worldly-wise, intelligent and experienced. Her descriptions of previous negotiations are filled with facts, balanced will charming anecdotes that take her opponents' focus off their own plans. She doesn't know if she would take no for an answer because she's never had to do so.

The womanly art of negotiating means adopting the best of style and substance of other female negotiators. Keep an open mind. Realize you can learn from women who differ from you in history, lifestyle and experience. I take the wisdom of Angela, age two and Martha, age 92, into heart, mind and conference rooms.

24 Role Play to Outwit Your Opponent

Excellent negotiators are dynamic actors. The act of role playing provides insights and confidence for real-life negotiations before they happen. Take on another person's persona by thinking, behaving and communicating as you imagine he would.

Role playing is especially effective when you are not feeling confident despite your excellent research and preparation. It is a method of breaking patterns of ineffective communication. This eye-opening strategy solves mysteries of slow-going, frustrating negotiations.

Uninhibitedly

Set your mind to enjoy being someone else. Role players are destined to underperform when they are anxious, embarrassed or self-absorbed. Let your serious side go. Done with the correct attitude: creativity flourishes; improvisational talents blossom; humor springs forth.

Switching Roles

You have opportunities to role play in a variety of configurations, such as: wife and husband switching roles to experience how differently females and males negotiate; team members in your corporate department switching places to look into and solve workplace conflicts; and board members switching authority to better understand policymaking from one another's point of view.

Step by Step

Basic role playing steps are identical in your professional and personal lives.

Identify a negotiating goal
Cast the players
Know yourself
Set the timeframe
Play uninhibitedly
Review what you've learned
Apply to real-life negotiation

The Outwit Your Opponent Scenario

You are Mr. Minor, owner of Minor Real Estate. Your opponent is Mr. Major, ceo of Major Enterprises, a larger real estate firm. Major wants to buy your company, but not for your price. Your goal is to examine interactions and determine what must change to close the deal.

In our role playing scenario, you are Mr. Major. You are played by Mr. Midway, your marketing director. The timeframe is set for 30 minutes roleplay, 15 minutes review.

You quickly discover that Midway has excellent abilities and no qualms about being you. He begins the discussion with an optimistic statement that you know you can come to terms today. But he speaks more softly, hesitatingly, and at a higher pitch than you think you do.

You boisturously demand that he proffer a better deal. The louder you get, the more intimidated Midway acts. You stand over him, waving the rejected sales document in his face, reading aloud key points of disagreement. Instead of standing in protest, Midway sinks deeper into his chair, avoiding eye contact and clearing his throat as if he'd like to say something, but can't.

You feel surprised about the strong feeling of power this takes over your body. Your tenor tones sound baritone. Your body language demonstrates standing tall, shoulders back, arms akimbo to maximum the space you take in the room. A mischievous grin appears on the your face as if to say *I know something you don't*. You aren't yourself – and you are very pleased.

As you and Mr. Midway review the scenario, emotions and aha! lessons arise. Your strength during the next negotiation with Mr. Major will be in playing the game, his way.

Looking Inward

Thelma and Louise (in their movie roles) delighted in role playing. Escaping their wifely duties in a dangerous, Chick Flick adventure, they tried to outpace police cars chasing them for suspected robbery and murder. No, they couldn't negotiate their way out of trouble and, as the movie climax reveals, drove off a cliff and into eternity. But not before they transformed themselves into women of confidence who had learned these lessons to role play effectively:

be unafraid to make mistakes
know you deserve to win;
be comfortable with spontaneity
release your all-or-nothing attitude
use setbacks to motivate, not procrastinate

Preemptive Strikes

The more intense and serious the negotiation, the more vital it is to face our fears, anger and self-doubts before starting to role play. Franklin Delanor Roosevelt admonished, "We have nothing to fear but fear itself." His wife Eleanor took her own excellent advice, "No one can make you feel inferior without your permission."

Give yourself the strategic advantages of striking preemptively to prepare for impending challenges: Role play.

25. Shakespeare's Playful Negotiations

As You Like It

"All the world's a stage,
And all the men and women merely players:
They have their exits and their entrances;
And one man in his time plays many parts."
(Jacques, monologue, Act II : Scene VII)

Life isn't always a romantic comedy affirming optimism, spousal fidelity and society-sanctioned behavior. In Shakespeare's *As You Like It*, the playfully positive Rosalind and the worldly-wise pessimist Jacques provide unique viewpoints as good triumphs over evil.

At the play's heart are the dramatic shenanigans of couples in love, separating, being socially tabu for each other, fleeing scenes of heated arguments. They bicker, banish and battle.

Negotiating well in such situations require:

Thinking and acting positively.
Communicating with opponents with respect and humor, although background, culture and world views differ.
Remembering we all play different roles at different times.
Being flexible in getting our points across and accepting our opponents' points.
Taking breaks from discussions when tempers explode and common sense isn't common.

King Lear

"Sir, I love you more than words can wield the matter.
Beyond what can be valued, rich or rare."
(Goneril, Eldest Daughter of King Lear, Act 1: Scene 1)

"Sir, I am made Of the selfsame metal that my sister is.
In my true heart I find she names my very deed of love."
(Regan, Middle Daughter of King Lear, Act I: Scene 1)

"What shall I speak? Love, and be silent.
Since I am sure my love's more richer than my tongue."
(Cordelia, Youngest Daughter of King Lear, Act 1: Scene 1)

We women have been twisting men around our little fingers since Eve met that snake. In Shakespeare's *King Lear*, the monarch is at the brink of stepping down from the throne dividing his kingdom equally among his three daughters.

Sisters Goneril and Regan crave his money and power. Throughout the play, they say and do all within their evil little minds to convince dad to hand over the castle keys and the moat passcode.

Cordelia (his favorite) plays the good daughter role, refusing to take part in the exuberant false flatteries spoken by her sisters, hoping Lear will see her true worth and reward her laid-back attitude. But this sisterly competitor seems uninterested. Lear, disappointed in Cordelia's lack of enthusiasm, splits his kingdom between Goneril and Regin.

One would think a wise king would have been leery of his daughters' false flatteries. When I performed Regan on stage, I realized the sisters' negotiating ploys go far beyond dysfunctional family relationships and provide patterns for modern-day negotiating techniques.

Lessons can be learned by carefully reviewing what worked and what backfired:

Insider knowledge.
Confidence in a father's never-ending love (or your competitor's respect for you.
Flattery, modesty and hubris.
Lack of morals.
Creative thinking.
Willingness to break old and create new rules.
Determination to 'Outwit, Outlast, Outplay' your competition ala tv's 'Survivor' series.
Honesty.

You may want to see or read the play, but I warn you, the ending isn't a happy example of win-win negotiations.

All's Well That Ends Well

"I am undone: there is no living, none.
If Bertram be away. 'Twere all one
That I should love a bright particular star.
And think to wed it, he is so above me."
(Helena, Act I: Scene I)

Noble-born, Bertram thinks socially-inferior, albeit passionately infatuated Helena isn't destined to be his bride. He treats her shabbily, with a pomposity that would discourage a less determined female. She responds by tricking him into getting her pregnant and evoking his wedding vows of love.

As *All's Well That Ends Well* ends, the audience (and, I'm certain, Helena) doubt this is the fairy tale ending she connived and cajoled to achieve.

What can negotiators learn from this play?

Think first. Think again. Only then speak.
Ask for what you want and want what you ask for.
Be willing to live with the negotations' results, especially if your goals evolved contrary to your best interests.
Know it is difficult to change yourself; You cannot change other people.
Maintain a healthy sense of self-respect and self-confidence.

Troilus and Cressida:
A Final Note from the Bard

"Things won are done, joy's soul lies in the doing."
(Cressida's Soliloquoy, Act I: Scene I)

26. Alice Negotiates in Wonderland

The next time you fall down a rabbit hole you will be prepared. Lewis Carroll's classic *Alice in Wonderland* and *Through the Looking Glass* sequel provide a plethora of imaginative and practical advice.

The book's spunky young heroine sets goals and thinks intensely about problems and solutions. Alice isn't fazed by the quirky characters she encounters.

She speaks her mind, takes action and remains steadfastedly optimistic. Take her insightful conversations to heart and mind and into practice.

Alice

"Alice generally gave herself very good advice, though she seldom followed it." In this instance, do the former – give yourself thoughtful advice – and have the confidence to follow it.

"What does it matter where my body happens to be?" said Alice. "My mind goes on working all the same. In fact, the more head downwards I am (falling down the rabbit hole), the more I keep inventing new things."

Honor your mental and physical states with control and courage. Celebrate inventing new things.

Cheshire Cat

One day Alice came to a fork in the road and saw a Cheshire Cat in a tree. "Which road do I take?" she asked. "Where do you want to go?" was his response. "I don't know," Alice answered. "Then," said the Cat, "it doesn't matter."

Make your negotiation matter, starting with a plan to pinpoint where, how and why you want to go. Prepare for roadblocks, traffic jams and accidents. The where, how and why you go may require changes as you move along. Be ready. Be flexible.

Red Queen

The Red Queen admonished Alice, "Always speak the truth. Think before you speak. Write it down afterwards."

I add this caveat: Speak the truth as you know it and will present it during negotiations. React truthfully to your opponent's questions, but do not give away information detrimental to you, beneficial to him.

"Sometimes I've believed as many as six impossible things before breakfast," said the Red Queen. Alice laughed. "There's no use trying," she said, "one can't believe impossible things

"I daresay you haven't had much practice," said the Queen. "When I was your age, I always did it for half an hour a day."

Creativity

Creativity (always a positive attribute for negotiators) requires believing in the impossible. Your right brain is pumping thoughts you (and perhaps no one else) has never come up with before.

This certainly doesn't mean they're impossible. It does mean they're worthy of further creativity to put them into action. The more you practice and pursue the good habit of creativity, the better your results.

Duchess

"If everybody minded their own business, the world would go around a great deal faster than it does," said the Duchess to Alice.

Deals would be negotiated more quickly and effectively to achieve win-win fruition. Mind your own business and keep a business mindset in all aspects of your negotiations.

"Tut, tut, child!" she scolded Alice. "When you've once said a thing, it's too late to correct it: You must take the consequences. Everything's got a moral, iyou can find it."

Organize your thoughts, take a deep breath, then open your mouth. You can find the moral of negotiating effectively by thinking about a negotiation that proved successful for you.

The King

"Begin at the beginning," the King said very gravely, "and go on till you come to the end: Then stop." The King went on, "I shall never, *never* forget!" "You will, though," the Queen said, "if you don't make a memorandum of it."

When a negotiation goes smoothly it is likely because you state your goals, focus on details and communicate confidently to closure. Making timely notes about why a negotiation worked well is in your own best interests.

Humpty Dumpty & March Hare

"When I use a word,"Humpty Dumpty said in rather a scornful tone, "it means just what I choose it to mean – neither more nor less." The question is," said Alice, "whether you *can* make words mean so many different things."

Say what you mean: Mean what you say. Paraphrase your opponents' statement to be certain you understand his points. Don't hesitate to ask questions.

Unicorn

"Well, now that we *have* seen each other," said the Unicorn, "if you'll believe in me, I'll believe in you. Is that a bargain?" "Yes, if you like," said Alice.

Believe in yourself, follow the *Wonderland* advice and you will be prepared next time you fall down a rabbit hole.

27. Negotiating Lessons from a Pawn Star

Pablo Picasso's etching of a dove. Tiffany & Company's Civil War-era sword. A lottery ticket signed by George Washington. These are among thousands of items negotiated by Rick Harrison. He is co-owner of the *Gold & Silver Pawn Shop* near the Las Vegas Strip and co-star of *Pawn Stars*, a History Channel reality show phenomenon.

Rick applies his natural abilities as an entrepreneur, psychologist, motivator, historian and humorist to create fascinating and informative life lessons in negotiating.

Using examples of his in-shop transactions, we'll examine the skills and techniques he relies on to turn treasures into profit.

Treasure Trove of Experts

Pristine 1940s Western movie posters. Gaudily glittering Rolex watches. Shipwreck-retrieved ancient Greek coins. Rick goes beyond relying on his copious knowledge of the world's treasure trove.

His support system of experts cover a broad range of esoteric specialties. They give accurate history, authenticate, declare rarity, and value for retail and auction house prices.

All this to the seller or pawner's delight or dismay.

Experts on the topics of your negotiations can heighten your credibility, confirm your asking price, and liase in communicating with your opponents.

Napoleon and Josephine
"Everything has a story and a price."

Rick is a voracious reader and scholar with a bursting curiosity about historical objects. Over the shows's opening credits, he intones, "I'm Rick Harrison and this is my pawn shop. I've learned everything in here has a story and a price. You never know what's going to come through that door."

Yes, every negotiation has a story and a price. Although you prepare as thoroughly as possible, you never know beforehand precisely how the negotiation will evolve. Your in-depth research and planning are your foundations for communicating your goals and presenting your strengths.

"I have no idea what their value is, but I want them," says Rick, into the camera, out of the hearing of the fellow who wants to sell handpainted miniature portraits of Napoleon and Josephine in ornate gold frames.

As the negotiation proceeds, it turns out that the customer hasn't done his research about the portraits' value. Rick consults with an expert, considers how much they'd tempt his clientele and makes an offer. The intimidated seller accepts and Rick's profit margin is assured.

Your opponent can't consider your counteroffer unless you make one. Timing is of the essence: Don't stop negotiating too early just because you're tired of the process. End the meeting, come back fresh and ask for what you want.

"Laugh and the World Laughs with You"
(from 'Solitude' by poet Ella Wheeler Wilcox)

While Rick's on his own turf, most sellers don't enter the shop filled with self-confidence and knowledge about their object's worth.

Rick takes them off-guard, greeting them with a casual, humorous comment. He knows making someone grin or gaffaw will lower the fellow's stress level and make him more amenable to win-win negotiating. One clever seller responded humorously, emphasizing that Rick is the only pawnbroker who'd appreciate his Pez dispenser collection.

Humorous interactions can evoke camaraderie and lessen tension by distracting participants from frustrating situations where minds don't meet.

"I'm all about creative solutions"

Man has gun: Man wants guitar. As Rick says, "I'm all about creative solutions." He offers to trade the fellow toting a 1750 French flintlock gun with bayonet for a classic 1978 Les Paul guitar. Rick's not out any money and the seller happily walks away with the instrument of his musical dreams.

How creative can you be during a negotiation? Be sure your well-honed plans to achieve your goals include flexibility. Creativity covers imaginative ways to coax your opponent into accepting an offer benefiting you both.

The Traditional Las Vegas Question:
Real or Fake?

Pawn shops are subject to scams by unscrupulus misanthropes. Rick rapidly evaluates his customer's appearance, demeanor and body language. "What do you know about this Rolex and why do you want to pawn it?" he asks.

He's suspicious when the fellow is overly nervous, claims history without provenance, and is anxious to deal quickly.

Pawn shops are decidedly open for folks who need quick cash. But their better part of wisdom isn't, of course, to announce, "The rent's due and I have no choice." When Rick asks, "What do you want for it?" they give the first number.

Sometimes folks who are certain they have a treasure end up devastated. "One of the hardest parts of my job is telling someone a prized family possession is a fake," says Rick.

Pity the woman who learned the hand-carved, ivory elephant tusk she bought on a safari vacation is plastic.

In negotiations, don't automatically presume your opponent is telling the truth.

Be thoughtful and careful about providing information. Ask yourself why you're revealing details that may benefit your opponent and harm you. Rein in your emotions.

Business Sense

Rick insists, "If it doesn't make sense, I'm not going to do it. This is a business. If I forget that for a second, I'm out of business."

Successful negotiators have the uncommon quality of common sense. We're in the business of knowing what we want and focusing on how to get it. We work and play intensely, fairly and determinedly to stay in business.

Negotiating Lessons Learned

Rick's success reflects his passion for negotiating professionally and fairly. He does his research, has a broad knowledge base, consults with experts, treats customers with respect and a sense of humor, communicates effectively, stands firm on his top price, and usually doesn't take himself too seriously.

He celebrates success with his *Silver & Gold Pawn Shop* cohorts, co-owner Richard (Old Man) Harrison, son Corey (Big Hoss) Harrison and family friend Austin (Chumlee) Russell.

Learn Rick's lessons and you'll have more success negotiating on and off the Las Vegas Strip.

28. Professional Negotiating Skills

You negotiate every day of your life. The word *negotiate* has its origin in the early 17th century: Latin *negotiat-* meaning 'done in the course of business.' It's the business of our lives -- not just our business lives -- to reach agreements and compromises through discussion. To resolve issues so all parties involved consider themselves winners. To graciously accept results when they are mutually fair and satisfactory.

Professional negotiators enjoy negotiating. We focus on researching, organizing and planning. Success enhances our self-confidence and motivates our optimism about future interactions. Wordplay and using our excellent verbal and written communication skills delight us. We use our time, energy and resources to full advantage.

Your Life Challenges

The identical negotiating skills, strategies and tactics apply to both your personal and professional lives. Yes, they differ in intensity, in how you communicate and in their emotional components, but success is sweet whether you are convincing your husband to buy a new car or motivating that rigid bank officer to give you his best loan terms.

Since our lives contain an everchanging myriad of negotiations, we can't overestimate the importance of setting priorities. Consider those all-too-often moments when you face the reality you can't accomplish everything you'd like to achieve. Professional negotiators develop a vibrant sense of logic leading to decisions benefiting all parties.

The classic Pareto Principal is one key to negotiating success: It is the rule that 20% of what you do helps you accomplish 80% of your goals. The rule can be expanded to reveal that 20% of how you invest your time and energy will result in an 80% success rate in using both wisely and productively.

Embrace the Pareto Principal to establish your true and essential negotiating goals. Commit to performing with a negotiator's mindset. Analyze the individual components of each goal to determine what actions, activities, resources and communications are essential on your path toward success.

The more you know about your own needs, wants, reasons and abilities – and those of your opponents – the better you will focus on mutually beneficial results.

In Praise of Practice

Even the most successful (perhaps, especially the most successful) negotiators know the importance of practicing the communications aspects of their art. Personal appearance, vocal intonations and body language serve as foundation for conveying carefully crafted messages in conversations, discussions and presentations.

Audio and video recordings of negotiation practice sessions, when reviewed and critiqued, lead to understanding how to improve your communication skills. Testing out your words by talking with and getting reactions from friends can save you from misguided negotiations with your spouse.

Roleplaying with colleagues can give you insights into what to keep and what to change when facing your opponents.

The Eternal Verities

Before you utter a single word to begin a negotiation, silently contemplate the eternal verities, those essential moral principals that make you who you are proud to be.

Remember that you are about to ask for what you want. Be certain that you want what you ask for.

Be willing to walk away, temporarily or permanently, but consider the people and circumstances involved before you take that first step. Requesting time to catch your breath, reconsider and think will dramatically benefit your outcome. Angry outbursts are anathema to positive results.

We professional negotiators prepare ourselves to seize moments of opportunity through detailed researching and planning. We are patient and forgiving with ourselves, our colleagues, even our opponents. We are willing to confess our mistakes, forgive ourselves, learn from them, offer apologies, start anew.

Magicians, Improvisors and Thespians

We've all been blessed with those days when the world is on our side. We are, in heart and mind, capable of being magicians, improvisors and thespians, in personal and professional negotiations.

Magic is not slight of hand, but the right words that suddenly transform your teenager's adamant *no* into a smiling *yes*.

NEGOTIATING FOR LIFE

It's the day you attended a conference and were invited at the very last minute to join the panel on the dais: Your cleverly improvised responses to audience questions secured potential clients.

Feeling a bit out of sorts, you followed the rule of always trying to be your best. To paraphrase Shakespeare, every conference room is a stage. You convinced yourself to act confidently and closed a deal far before deadline.

Professional negotiators celebrate every victory – personal and professional, miniscule and major.

29. Realities of Positive Negotiating

I'm convinced every pessimistic, frustrated and sarcastic negotiator has a nemisis: A positive thinker of good-intentioned mind who will drive him crazy.

Successful negotiators thrive on positive attitudes. As a born optimist, I've focused energy to convince innate pessimists to join the lighter side. Sharing the purpose-driven march toward joyful enlightment has evoked scoff, rejection and doubt. These have led me to examine the realities of positive negotiating.

Buddha

Opening my front door, an 18th-century Buddha statue greets me. She is strong of stone and beatific of face. Her welcome home serenity gives me feelings of positive energy, no matter the day's challenges. I decide to embrace her positive momentum. Switching to a negative mindset contains neither plan nor purpose.

You -- in the roles of negotiator and motivator, communicator and persuader -- interpret facts, potentials and probabilities. Naturally, your mood and mindset will influence how well you perform.. Adopting Buddhist qualities of calm mind, concentration and control are the equivalent of allowing images of a gentle stream flow through your positive thoughts, carrying them into your body.

Questioning "What's best for me...in this situation, with these people, in solving a problem?" is always worth asking and answering honestly. More often than not, the positive approach contributes to mental, physical and emotional health and best possible negotiating outcomes.

Cattle Flight Zone

The calves in my herd are cautiously optimistic and physically self-protective. Craving a trough filled with protein mix, they respond with kindergartners' exuberance at snacktime. They quickly approach as I sing *Amazing Grace*, listening as I empty the bucket and wish them bon appetit.

Feeding time is always an exercise in negotiating. With cattle, a *flight zone* is defined as how close they'll allow humans to come before the animals walk or run away just enough for them to feel safe.

Their goal is to eat without fear. My goal is to get close enough to check their health, ear identification tags, and interactions with each other.

Humans need flight zones with other humans. A positive attitude and acknowledging when to close in or to step back improve all aspects of the relationship between human and beast -- and between human and human.

Stepping back gives a difference perspective to a situation, one that may change the course of its outcome for the better.

Anger

Our appearance and body language are important factors in negotiating. Consider the negotiation that reaches its peak of anger. Business jackets are shucked off, ties thrown on the table. The result is a dramatic, it's damn hot in here, little chance to get down to business setting. Grimaces and tightened body parts bring discomfort.

Anger has no place in thinking positively. It is not the way to control ourselves or our situations. Turned inward, it is debilitating and stressful. Turned outward, it is an invitation for everyone involved to lose focus, attention and credibility.

The positive negotiator seeks balance. She knows the value of taking time to reconsider the scheduled timing of discussions and decisions.

Devil's Advocate

An unbridled positive attitude can be so disruptive that your opponents and your own negotiating team will harken to times of quiet desperation instead of cooperation. They may instantly take the devil's advocate stance, arguing and exploring the opposite of every idea anyone puts forth. Their response to your I've-got-it-under-control position is to find your weak spots, illogical points, and meanderings into the too-good-to-be-true environs.

Control

So much of our lives is out of control. Why not take the opportunity to take control when we are able to do so?

NEGOTIATING FOR LIFE

Every negotiation situation fluctuates and is unpredictable because people fluctuate and are unpredictable. Even the cast of characters involved may change their minds, be replaced by others, or become beneficiaries or victims of external circumstances.

We show self-respect and logic when we make the conscious decision to have a positive attitude.

Fate

Much to our chagrin, bad things happen to good people. Even worse, good things happen to bad people. *'The fate is not in our stars, but in ourselves,"* wrote Shakespeare. No offence to the Bard, but life is not perfectly fair no matter how hard we try to make it so.

All we can do is to do all we can to make it fair: Positive does not mean perfect.

30. Believing in Negotiating

Believing in your negotiating abilities is a fine way to believe in yourself.

Major successful negotiations can prove frustratingly anticlimactic, as tiny failed negotiations can evoke cataclismic reactions. Thinking all-or-nothing, black-or-white is a dangerous way to proceed. Positive self-confidence without going to contemplative extremes fosters negotiating success.

Kindergartner's Political Advice

My friend Julie was running for her kindergarten's presidency. Your first reaction may be that our school systems are pushing our younguns ahead far too quickly. Her mom and dad had tried to discourage her from running, fearful losing might devastate her.

Julie had her political negotiating ducks in a row. With a broad smile, exuberant body language, and a heartfelt declaration, she convinced them. "I will be the best kindergarten class president. I know what we kids need. I know how to talk to grownups. And, anyway, some of the other kids don't even know their alphabets." The latter was a sly way of complimenting her parents, who encouraged literacy at a young age. They acquiesced.

As another loving adult in Julie's life, I decided to encourage her political aspirations. She requested a mock interview to prepare her to communicate more effectively than her opponents. Actually, Julie said, "JB, could you ask me a coupla (sic) questions to get me more ready?"

She had already polished her platform. Longer snacktimes. More computer access. Additional storytime readalouds.

All I could think of to ask was, "Julie, how do you plan to win this important election?" She grinned, then replied in a serious tone indicative of no less than a second grader, "JB, you always have to vote for yourself."

The Lord Above, in Song

You'd be surprised by what we choir members don't wear under our robes. T-shirts emblazoned *Keep Calm & Carry On.* Weight Watcher devotees in tank tops and short shorts. Lacily see-through Victoria Secret matching unmentionables. It's damn hot under our white cottas and ankle-length black cassocks.

Our choir director has the patience of a proverbial saint. She is highly skilled in all the steps of negotiating. She shares her goals for and with us in a well-honed plan. Show up for practices. Memorize hymns and anthems to perform *off-book.* Keep our bodies healthy and our voices in well-toned shape. Give our all with spiritual enthusiasm to make her proud. She accepts the reality that our physical comfort is non-negotiable.

Negotiating is about setting and keeping true to our priorities. We sing to her (and we hope the Lord's) satisfaction. The congregation is clueless about the wardrobe issue.

Environmental Affairs

I believe negotiating is essential to assure a beautiful, safe and productive world for ourselves and for generations to come. Counting myself and my husband among active environmentalists, we share our dedication, views, and intellectual and financial commitments with thousands of our fellow North Carolinians.

Working with likeminded souls, we carefully focus on the basic steps of negotiating. These include researching the issues, gathering information about our opponents, and formulating plans and communications with our colleagues before we take action. The best action is meaningful negotiation, not confrontation.

Corporate exccutives, politicians and advocacy groups often have different agenda from ours. Their priority is money. Taking chances on the future of the earth is their bailiwick. Their activities produce toxic chemicals that make clean, drinkable water unsafe and undrinkable. What they do not know about the consequences of fracking on our water, air and health could fill all of *Wikipedia*.

6 NEGOTIATING FOR LIFE

It is difficult to communicate with our opponents. It is a as clear to us as the water flowing through an unmolested stream, that logic demands we protect the earth and her inhabitants. Moving to a state of negotiation opens the path to meaningful resolutions.

Perserverance is a precious power. It keeps lines of communication open, and attracts particpation by more and more people who believe as we do. It is always worth fighting/negotiating when issues involve negative actions that, once done, can never be undone.

We negotiate with head and heart, purpose and passion. As you negotiate your way through life, may these attributes bring you success after success.

***

www.ingramcontent.com/pod-product-compliance
Lightning Source LLC
Chambersburg PA
CBHW072024040426
42447CB00009B/1727